Rethinking the Wineskin

OTHER BOOKS BY FRANK VIOLA

**Visit the Present Testimony Ministry Web Site for
Free Downloads and Ordering Information:**

www.ptmin.org

RETHINKING THE WINESKIN

The Practice of the
New Testament Church

Frank Viola

RETHINKING THE WINESKIN:
THE PRACTICE OF THE NEW TESTAMENT CHURCH

Third Edition

Copyright © 2001 by Present Testimony Ministry

Published by
Present Testimony Ministry
ptmin@aol.com / www.ptmin.org

Printed in the United States of America

This book is dedicated to a beautiful girl who lives in Brandon, Florida. This corporate woman embodies the truths found in this book. By her life, she proves them to be heavenly realities and not the theories of men.

CONTENTS

FOREWORD

Frank Viola's *Rethinking the Wineskin* is part of a long, distinguished line of expositions portraying the way of life that characterized the NT (New Testament) church and its effect on us today. Voices like Frank's express the distinctiveness of the first-century church. The church is a body, a family, and a bride. In effect, the NT church is *relational*.

That the NT church is relational is itself uncontroversial. Yet for many people, books like Frank's come as a shock. The churches most of us inhabit have little or nothing in common with the way of life that marked the early church.

Far from being a body or a family, the church for most of us is an organization or an institution. The contrast between the institutional shape of the contemporary church and the relational shape of the first-century church could hardly be more striking.

The institutional church often knows, at least vaguely, that the NT church was a very different kind of beast. Yet it goes on its way in blithe disregard of the way the early believers were church. It may even claim that the Bible is its sole authority in "faith and practice" and still virtually ignore its practical authority with respect to church practice.

Maybe that is by choice. But most often the ignorance is due to momentum. Institutional churches are a lot like trains. They are going in a certain direction, and they will continue in that direction for a good long time even if all hands try to make them stop.

As with trains, the options for turning the direction of institutional churches are limited at best. If a switch or siding is available, the train could turn. Otherwise, it just follows its tracks. So everyone aboard had best hope that he is on the right train headed in the right direction.

Relational churches, like those in the NT, are different. They are not trains, but groups of people out for a walk. They move much more slowly than trains—only several miles per hour at the fastest. But they can turn at a moment's notice. More importantly, they can be genuinely attentive to their world, to their Lord, and to each other.

Like trains, institutional churches are easy to find. The smoke and noise are unmistakable. Relational churches are a bit more subtle. Because they do not announce their presence with flashing lights at every intersection, some believe that churches like those in the NT died out long ago. But nothing could be farther from the truth.

Relational churches are everywhere. I personally have been meeting with one for more than twenty years. Still, groups like ours are quietly walking together, not bothering to call undue attention to ourselves. We are simply pilgrims together.

Yet once you learn how to spot a relational church, you will soon discover groups of people everywhere meeting just like the NT church. As bodies, families, and brides rather than as institutions. I personally know of scores of them. Those groups collectively know of hundreds or thousands more.

They are simply groups of people walking with God. The trains pass them by all the time. Sometimes the people on board wave. Sometimes they cannot because the train is moving so fast that people going a few miles per hour just look like a blur.

But all this is within Frank's book. His approach is his own—*didactic* and *spiritual* at the same time. This allows him to unfold the NT church and its effect on us in a distinctive fashion.

If you are in one of the groups of people now walking around as a relational church, *Rethinking the Wineskin* will give you a new appreciation of your roots in the NT. If you are on one of the trains whizzing by, it may be a bit surprising to find out that some of those blurred patches of color outside your window are groups of people walking with God. That thing you just passed was another relational church.

Hal Miller
Salem, Massachusetts

PREFACE TO THE FIRST EDITION

In the following pages I have sought to revisit the provocative question of how we do church in the 20th century. My intent has been two-fold: 1) to introduce the Biblical vision of first-century church life to those who are unfamiliar with it, and 2) to cultivate a deeper understanding of how the practice of the church relates to God's ultimate intention.

Throughout this book, I will be referring to those churches with which most people are familiar as "institutional churches." I could have just as easily called them "establishment churches," "basilica churches," "traditional churches," "organized churches," "clergy-dominated churches," "contemporary churches," or "program-based churches." All are inadequate linguistic tools. Yet to my mind, "institutional church" best captures the essence of most assemblies today.

A sociologist may object to my use of the word "institutional." Sociologically speaking, an institution is any patterned human activity. Thus a handshake and a greeting hug are institutions. I readily admit that all churches (even the ones I endorse) assume some institutions.

But I am using the phrase "institutional church" in a much narrower sense. Namely, I am referring to those churches that operate primarily as institutions that exist above, beyond, and independent of their individual members. Such churches are organizationally centered on professional pastors and staff. They are constructed on programs more than relationships. And they are unified on the basis of special doctrines (teachings) or practices.

By contrast, this book promotes a vision of the church that is organic in its construction. Relational in its functioning. Scriptural in its form. Christ-centered in its operation. And Body-oriented in its unification. Stated simply, the purpose of this book is to discover afresh what it means to be *church* from God's standpoint.

If you have never read anything that challenged your notion of "church," this book will explode like a bombshell. If you are not yet ready to make an honest and rigorous appraisal of the contemporary church, this explosion will prove offensive.

On the other hand, if you are daring enough to bring every practice under the scrutiny of Biblical revelation. If you are willing to step out of the safe limits of traditional religion. And if you are prepared to spurn compromise, the explosive truths presented in this book will liberate you into a new dimension of spiritual reality.

I am aware that a plethora of books has already been written on the early church. They crowd the shelves of seminary libraries and used-book stores. Some may wonder, therefore, why I see the need to add another one to the lot.

Quite simply, I believe the value of this book lies chiefly in its approach. That is, it seeks to combine both the *heavenly* and *spiritual* nature of God's eternal purpose with the *practical* and *earthly* dimensions of church life.

A few books have sought to discuss the former in the light of the latter. Sadly, many of them have gone out of print. But this book seeks to present the latter through the lens of the former.

It thoroughly explores the practice of the early church within the context of the eternal purpose of God. It also attempts to preserve a healthy balance between the church's *theological* aspect and its *practical* aspect. Stated simply, this book is a modest attempt to present old truths from fresh angles.

I will shamelessly admit that I am no expert in ecclesiology (the theological study of the church). What I have written has come out of my own Biblical search. It has also grown out of my experience in meeting with churches that gather in the manner that this book describes. Thus this work is not theoretical. It has been birthed by spiritual vision and walked out in Christian shoe leather.

What I offer in these pages is not the polished work of a professional scholar. It is rather the roughly-hewn labor of an ordinary believer who has both re-thought and re-practiced the church for over a decade. Because this is not a scholarly treatise, I have chosen to cite my sources informally. The major publications I quote from are listed in an extensive bibliography at the end of the book.

I offer this book as part of the ongoing work of the Master Builder, the Lord Jesus Christ, who continues to build His church with the living stones of the redeemed.

Frank A. Viola
Brandon, Florida
January 1997

PREFACE TO THE THIRD EDITION

It has been five years since the original edition of *Wineskin* was published. Since that time, the book has caused quite a stir in the Christian world. In his mercy, God has chosen to use it to open the eyes of countless saints to behold the elegant simplicity of the first-century church. As a result, many have left the walls of institutional Christianity to become part of something higher.

Thankfully, the book remains to be in high demand. At the time of this revision, *Wineskin* has been translated into eight languages. Given the increasing circulation of the book, I felt burdened to improve certain features.

First, I have lowered the reading level in order to broaden my audience. I wrote the first edition on an 11th grade level. The new edition you hold in your hands is easier to plug through. It is written at a 9th grade level. Special thanks goes to Susan Groulx and Mike Biggerstaff for their tremendous editing work.

Second, I have tightened and clarified several sections of the book to prevent misunderstanding. This edition reads cleaner and clearer than the original. I have also added a short appendix at the end that answers the oft-repeated question: "What do I do now that I have seen that the institutional church is unscriptural?"

Third, this new addition sports a nicer cover. The other books I plan to write on Christ and the church will be clothed in similar covers—thus making a handsome series.

Fourth, I wish to alert my readers that throughout this book I use the terms "NT church," "early church," and "first-century church" as synonyms. All of these terms refer to the early church of Century One as it is portrayed in the NT.

Fifth, since the first penning of this book five years ago, I have gotten involved in the work of planting first-century styled churches. Some of the insights I have gleaned from this experience, therefore, have been added to the book. This makes for a richer treatment of the subjects I deal with.

Finally, I suggest that those who read this book also obtain a copy of my on-line manuscript, *From Nazareth to Patmos: The Saga of the Early Church*. This book tells the entire story of the early church in chronological order. And it does so under one cover.

Rethinking the Wineskin is based on that very story. The difference is that *Wineskin* takes certain frames from that grand saga and divides them up into specific categories. Both books give the reader a portrait of the first-century church from two different vantage points.

I am confident that you will enjoy this new edition. And I trust it will ignite in you a passion for the restoration of God's beloved house—the church of the Lord Jesus Christ!

Frank A. Viola
Brandon, Florida
August 2001

INTRODUCTION

THE CALL FOR A NEW WINESKIN

No one sews a patch of unshrunk cloth on an old garment, for the patch will pull away from the garment, making the tear worse. Neither do men pour new wine into old wineskins. If they do, the skins will burst, the wine will run out and they will ruin the wineskins. No, they pour new wine into new wineskins, and they preserve both. (Matt. 9:16-17, NIV)

The theme of "church renewal" sits lavishly upon the tongues of countless Christians today. You cannot go very far in the Christian world without hearing an exhortation on the following: Unity in the Body of Christ. The priesthood of all believers. The destruction of all man-made barriers. Apostolic power and gifts. World-wide evangelism.

While none of these themes are new or original, they are now capturing the attention of many modern Christians. These currents of spiritual renewal are not exclusively flowing from any one stream of the Body of Christ. They are being heralded across denominational lines. Such Biblical accents of church renewal reflect the genuine stirring of God's Spirit through His people. They are channels of the wine. Even the *new wine* of the Holy Spirit.

Yet the testimony of the Spirit is also registering something else. Something that touches a deeper note. Through a quieter, yet no less fervent voice, God is challenging His beloved Bride to freshly examine the very *context* in which she experiences spiritual renewal.

Surfacing on the religious horizon, there can be detected a largely hidden, yet growing stream of ordinary Christians. And

God is using them to summon His people back to the simplicity and vitality of the early church.

The present burden of the Spirit is fastened upon securing a people who will shed their man-made, encrusted traditions concerning church leadership, church practice, and church organization. His burden is to have a people who will hand the church back to the complete mastery of the Lord Jesus Christ! Put another way, the Spirit is not only speaking about the *wine*. He is also speaking about the *wineskin*.

The present stream which stresses spiritual renewal and apostolic power is indeed genuine, and it preserves a Biblical insight. Yet this other "River of life," whose distinct chord is the recovery of apostolic practice and life, is cutting deeper channels toward God's eternal purpose.

Although the latter is less obvious than the former, it reflects the deepest yearnings of the blessed Savior for His Bride. To be blunt, there can be no full recovery of apostolic power if there is not first a recovery of apostolic life and practice!

Church history is rife with examples demonstrating that every past renewal has repackaged the new wine into old wineskins. By the old wineskin, I mean those traditional structures that are patterned after the old Judaic religious system. A system that separated God's people into two separate classes; required the presence of human mediators; erected sacred buildings; and laid stress on outward forms.

The facets of the old wineskin are many. The clergy/laity distinction. The spectator-performer styled church meeting. The single pastor system. The program-driven worship service. The passive priesthood. The edifice complex. All of these features represent Old Covenant forms in NT garb!

Accordingly, the present cry of the Spirit for genuine renewal will never become a reality for those who ignore His concurrent voice regarding the new wineskin. God Himself fashioned this fresh wineskin. He made it to perfectly hold the wine of His life. In this way, the wine *always* precedes the wineskin.

Sadly, not a few have presumed that God has left the wineskin of church practice to the pragmatic whims of well-intentioned men. But the Lord has not left us to ourselves concerning the practice of *His* church.

We so often forget that the church belongs to Christ and not to us! As in the Old Testament type, no peg of the tabernacle was left to the imagination of man. Rather, the house was to be built "according to the pattern" given from above.

This does not mean that the NT supplies us with an ironclad, meticulous blueprint for church practice. It does not. Therefore, it is a gross mistake to tease out of the apostolic letters an inflexible code of church order that is as unalterable as the law of the Medes and Persians! Such a written code belongs to the other side of the cross.

On the other hand, the NT introduces us to a number of clearly defined *practices* that characterize God's spiritual house. And it is these practices that make up the "Divine pattern" for the *ekklesia* (church).

Herein lies the aim of this book. It is an attempt to furnish us with a portrait of the original wineskin. The same wineskin that God shaped to contain His new wine. Each chapter paints a picture of the church as it is depicted on the canvas of the NT. And undergirding each brush stroke is a solemn plea for the sovereign rights of the Lord Jesus Christ in His house.

Let us not be so foolish to presume that if we retain the old wineskins of our liking that we will be able to preserve the new wine of the Spirit. As our Lord declared, when men put new wine into old wineskins, "the skins will burst and the wine will run out."

CHAPTER 1

THE CHURCH MEETING

The great Bible expositor Martyn Lloyd-Jones once said, "We are living in an age hopelessly below the NT pattern—content with a neat little religion." Holding that thought, I would like to begin our discussion on the practice of the NT church by examining *why* the early Christians gathered.

The Bible records a number of different kinds of Christian meetings. Among them are prayer meetings, evangelistic meetings, ministry meetings, apostolic meetings, and church meetings. In this chapter, we will look at the church meeting. By "church meeting," I refer to the main meeting of the church that is described in 1 Corinthians 11-14.

Before we explore the purpose of the church meeting, let us first explore why most Christians gather for "church" today. There are basically four reasons:

1) corporate worship,
2) evangelism,
3) hearing sermons, or
4) fellowship

As strange as it may seem, the NT *never* envisions any of these reasons as being the purpose of the church meeting.

The Place of Worship, Evangelism, Sermonizing, and Fellowship

According to the NT, worship is something we live. It is the setting forth of the thankfulness, affection, devotion, humility, and sacrificial obedience that God deserves at every moment (Matt. 2:11; Rom. 12:1; Phil. 3:3). When we gather together, we should come in a spirit of worship. But worship extends beyond our meetings.

For many Christians, worship is the equivalent of singing choruses, hymns, and praise songs. (Many mistakenly call this "praise and worship.") While worshiping God through song was an important expression of the early church meeting (Eph. 5:19; Col. 3:16), it was never its chief aim. Again, worship goes far beyond singing.

Likewise, the Bible never equates the purpose of the church meeting with evangelism. The NT demonstrates that evangelism commonly occurred outside the meetings of the church. The apostles preached the gospel in those places where unbelievers frequented. The synagogues (for the Jews) and the market places (for the Gentiles) were among their favorite places to evangelize (Acts 14:1; 17:1-33; 18:4,19).

By contrast, the NT church gathering was primarily a *believers* meeting. The context of 1 Corinthians 11-14 makes this quite plain. While unbelievers were sometimes present, they were not the focus of this meeting. (In 1 Corinthians 14:23-25, Paul fleetingly mentions the presence of unbelievers in the meeting.)

In this regard, the notion that the church meeting is for the sake of hearing sermons is without Biblical warrant. The saints certainly shared Christ in the early church gatherings. (1 Cor. 14 speaks of those bringing teachings, revelations, and prophecies.) But hearing "a sermon" was utterly foreign to the first-century believers.

In today's Protestant church service the pulpit is the central feature. Everything leads up to and is structured around the sermon. In fact, the congregation evaluates the meeting by the sermon's quality. Yet the NT cannot sustain this. The notion of a sermon-oriented, pulpit-pew styled church service was alien to the early Christians.

The apostles did preach the Word of God at length in certain settings. But these settings were not "church meetings."

They were "ministry meetings" designed for evangelistic purposes (or for the equipping of the church). These meetings would be akin to the special seminars, workshops, and conferences of our day. They should not be confused with "church meetings."

In the ministry meeting, workers share with an interactive audience, preaching Christ and equipping the saints for works of service. The twelve apostles held such meetings in Jerusalem (Acts 5:40-42). Paul held them in the Hall of Tyrannus when he was in Ephesus (Acts 19:9-10; 20:27,31).

In the church meeting, every member freely shares Christ (1 Cor. 14:26-40). No one takes center stage. Unlike today's practice, the teaching in the church meeting was not delivered by the same person week after week. Instead, every member had both the right and the privilege to minister Christ in the gathering.

Fellowship was not the main purpose of the gathering either. While fellowship is a demand of Body life, it was not the primary purpose of the early church meeting. Fellowship is simply one of the many organic outgrowths that emerge when God's people joyfully enthrone the Lord Jesus (Acts 2:42). Yet as necessary as fellowship is to the life of the church, we should not equate it with the purpose of the church meeting.

Mutual Edification

If the purpose of the first-century church meeting was not for corporate worship, evangelism, sermonizing, or fellowship, what was it for?

According to Scripture, the governing purpose of the church meeting is *mutual edification*. 1 Corinthians 14:26 puts it plainly:

What is the outcome then, brethren? WHEN YOU AS-SEMBLE, EACH ONE has a psalm, has a teaching, has a revelation, has a tongue, has an interpretation. Let all things be done for EDIFICATION. (NASB)

Hebrews 10:24-25 puts it even plainer:

And let us consider how to STIMULATE ONE ANOTHER to love and good deeds, not forsaking our own assembling together, as is the habit of some, but ENCOURAGING ONE ANOTHER, and all the more, as you see the day drawing near. (NASB, see also Rom. 14:19; 1 Thess. 5:11; and Heb. 3:13-14)

The meeting of the church envisioned in Scripture allowed for *every member* to participate in the building up of the Body (Eph. 4:16). Mutual encouragement was the hallmark of the gathering. "Every one of you" was its most outstanding characteristic.

While the early Christians worshiped God through song, they did not confine their singing to the leadership of a special group of "professional" musicians! Instead, the meeting allowed for "every one" to lead a song. In the words of Paul, "every one of you has a psalm" in the gathering.

Even the songs themselves were marked by an element of mutuality. Paul exhorts the brethren to "speak to *yourselves*, teaching and admonishing *one another* in psalms, hymns, and spiritual songs" (Eph. 5:19; Col. 3:16). In such an open format, the early Christians regularly composed their own songs and sang them in the meeting.

In like manner, each believer who possessed a word from the Lord had the liberty to supply it through his or her unique gift. A typical first-century meeting may have looked like this: The saints raise the roof with their singing. The group as a whole leads the singing. Each saint offers a prayer. A child shares a Bible story through a skit. A young woman gives her testimony.

Another sister reads a poem she wrote to express Christ's love toward His Bride. A single brother gives an exhortation interlaced with group interaction. An older, married brother expounds a portion of Scripture and follows it up with a prayer. A married sister tells a story out of her own spiritual experience. Several teenagers share what Christ showed them of Himself during a time of prayer they had earlier. The whole group experiences table fellowship as they take the Lord's Supper.

As Paul pulls back the curtain of the first-century gathering in 1 Corinthians 11-14, we see a meeting where every member is actively involved. Freshness, openness, and spontaneity are the chief marks of this meeting. Mutual edification is its primary goal.

Christ, the Director of the NT Gathering

All the Biblical examples about the church meeting solidly rest upon the Headship of Jesus Christ. This is the focal point of God's eternal purpose (Eph. 1:9-22; Col. 1:16-18). Christ was fully preeminent in the early church meeting. He was its Center and its Circumference. He set the agenda. He directed what took place. Although His leading was invisible to the naked eye, He was clearly the Guiding Agent.

The Lord Jesus was free to speak through whomever He chose. And in whatever capacity He saw fit. Consequently, the common practice of a few professional ministers assuming all the important activities of the church, while the rest of the saints remain passive, was utterly foreign to the early church.

The NT church meeting was based upon the "round-table" principle. That is, every member was encouraged to function. The institutional church is built on the "pulpit-pew" principle. It divides the members into the active few and the passive many.

In the first-century gathering, neither the sermon nor "the preacher" were the center. Instead, congregational participation was the Divine rule. The meeting was non-liturgical, non-ritualistic, and non-sacral. Nothing was sacrosanct. Nothing was perfunctory. Everything came out of life.

The meeting reflected a flexible spontaneity where the Spirit of God was in utter control. Jesus Christ was free to move through any member of His Body as He willed. And since He was leading the meeting, everything was done in an orderly fashion.

In fact, the Holy Spirit so governed the early church gathering that if a person received an insight while another was sharing, the second speaker was free to interject his thought (1 Cor. 14:29-30). Moreover, group interaction was a common part of the gathering (1 Cor. 14:27-40).

Such a meeting is unthinkable in the institutional church. Most Christians fear trusting the leadership of the Spirit to direct and shape their church services. The fact that they cannot envision a corporate gathering without placing themselves under the direct guidance of a human moderator shows that they are strangers to God's ways.

Much of the reason for this has to do with our own unfamiliarity with the Spirit's working in our personal affairs. If we do not know the Spirit's control in our own life, how can we know it when we gather together?

The truth is that many of us—like Israel of old—still clamor for a king to rule over us. We want a visible mediator to tell us what "God hath said" (Exod. 20:19; 1 Sam. 8:19). Regrettably, the presence of a human moderator in a Christian gathering is a cherished tradition to which most believers are fiercely committed. But it does not square with Scripture. Far worse, it suppresses Christ's Headship.

Nowhere in the NT do we find grounds for a church meeting that is dominated, directed, or facilitated by a human being. Neither do we find a gathering that is rooted in a pulpit centrality focused upon one man.

In fact, the most startling characteristic of the early church meeting was the absence of any human officiation. Jesus Christ led the meetings by the medium of the Holy Spirit through the believing community. The result? The spirit of "one-another-ing" pervaded the entire gathering. Mutuality was its unique seal. It is no wonder that the NT uses the phrase *one another* nearly sixty times. Watchman Nee observes,

> *In the church meetings, 'each one hath a psalm, hath a teaching, hath a revelation, hath a tongue, hath an inter-pretation' (1 Cor. 14:26). Here it is not a case of one leading and all others following, but each one contributing his share of spiritual helpfulness . . . man determines nothing, and each takes part as the Spirit leads. It is not an 'all man' ministry, but a Holy Ghost ministry . . . An opportunity is given to each member of the church to help others, and an opportunity is given to each one to be helped. One brother may speak at one stage of the gath-ering and another later on; you may be chosen of the Spirit to help the brethren this time, and I next time . . . Each individual must bear his share of responsibility and pass on to the others what he himself has received of the Lord. The conduct of the meetings should be the burden of no one individual, but all the members should bear the burden together, and they should seek to help one another de-pending upon the teaching and leading of the Spirit, and depending upon His empowering too . . . A church meeting has the stamp of 'one another' upon it. (The Normal Christian Church Life)*

Today's popular one-man orientation rivals the functional Headship of Christ. By contrast, each member of the early church came to the meeting knowing he or she had the priv-ilege and the responsibility to contribute something of Christ. An open freedom and informality marked the gathering.

Note that the idea of mutual ministry envisioned in the NT is a far cry from the pinched definition of "lay-ministry" that is promoted in the modern church. Most organized churches offer a surplus of volunteer positions for "laypeople" to fill. Positions like cutting the lawn of the parsonage. Ushering the aisles. Washing the pastor's car. Shaking hands at the sanctuary door. Passing out bulletins. Teaching Sunday school. Singing in the choir. Leading the worship team. Flipping transparencies.

But these restricted positions are light years away from the free-and-open exercise of spiritual gifts that was afforded to every believer in the early church gathering.

The Necessity of a Functioning Priesthood

So why did the early church meet in this way? Was it just a passing cultural tradition? Did it, as some say, represent the early church's infancy, ignorance, and immaturity? Never! The early church meeting is deeply rooted in Biblical theology. It made real and practical the NT doctrine of the priesthood of all believers—a doctrine that all evangelicals affirm with their lips.

And what is this doctrine? In the words of Peter, it is the teaching that all believers are spiritual priests called to offer up "spiritual sacrifices" unto the Lord. In Paul's language, it is the idea that all Christians are *functioning* members of the Body of Christ.

From a pragmatic standpoint, the early church meeting is the Biblical dynamic that produces spiritual growth—both corporately and individually (Eph. 4:11-16). We grow into God's fullness when the different parts of His Body minister Christ to us (Eph. 3:16-19). We also grow when we function (Mark 4:24-25).

Granted, believers can and should function outside the church meetings. But the gatherings of the church are especially designed for every Christian to express Christ through his or her gift (1 Cor. 11-14; Heb. 10:24-25). The institutional church commonly pushes "one anothering" outside of the church service. But this retards the growth of the believing community. For this reason, the institutional church is essentially a nursery for overgrown spiritual babes. It habituates God's people into being passive receivers. It stunts their spiritual development and keeps them in spiritual infancy. (The incessant need for predigested, dished out spiritual food is a mark of spiritual immaturity—1 Cor. 3:1-2; Heb. 5:12-14.)

The Reformation recovered the truth of the priesthood of all believers. But it failed to restore the necessary practices that embody this teaching. The church has *claimed* the ground of a believing priesthood. But it failed to *occupy* that ground!

In the typical Protestant church, the doctrine of the priesthood of all believers is no more than a sterile truth. Joseph Higginbotham and Paul Patton pointedly remark,

Every year on 'Reformation Sunday' it is urgently proclaimed that the Reformation won the battle for the priesthood of the believer. The wish is certainly the father of the thought, but we are still talking about wishes, not facts. The very congregations who hear this proclamation deny by their polity, their congregational life, and even by their architecture the truth they claim to embody . . . Our words betray our Reformation Sunday victory celebrations. The battle is not won; we do not yet occupy the ground where the priesthood of the believers is fact. ("The Battle for the Body," Searching Together, Vol. 13:2)

The truth of the believing priesthood in modern evangelicalism continues to beg for practical application and implementation in the life of the Lord's people. God has established open participatory meetings to incarnate the glorious reality of expressing Christ through a fully-employed priesthood.

God designed the early church meeting to fulfill His eternal purpose. A purpose centered on forming Christ in a company of people. A purpose centered on bringing them into His fullness (Gal. 4:19; Eph. 4:11-16).

Significantly, there is nothing more conducive to the culture of spiritual life than the open meeting that is depicted in the NT. The book of Hebrews amply demonstrates that the mutual supply of the Body is vital for the spiritual increase of every member.

Mutual ministry is the Divine *antidote* for preventing apostasy; the Divine *requirement* for ensuring perseverance; and the Divine *means* for cultivating individual spiritual life. Consider Hebrews 3:12-14:

> *Take heed, brethren, lest there be in any of you an EVIL HEART OF UNBELIEF, IN DEPARTING FROM THE LIVING GOD. BUT EXHORT ONE ANOTHER DAILY. . . LEST ANY OF YOU BE HARDENED THROUGH THE DECEITFULNESS OF SIN. For we are made partakers of Christ, if we hold the beginning of our confidence stedfast unto the end.*

Here we are told that mutual edification is the remedy for an unbelieving heart and a deceived mind. Similarly, in Hebrews 10:24-26, mutual encouragement is presented to us as the Divine safeguard against willful sin:

> *And let us consider how to STIMULATE ONE ANOTHER to love and good deeds, not forsaking our own assembling together, as is the habit of some, but ENCOURAGING ONE ANOTHER, and all the more, as you see the day drawing near. For if we go on sinning willfully after receiving the knowledge of the truth . . . (NASB).*

While multitudes of clergy have made common use of this text to stress the importance of "attending church," they have blissfully ignored the rest of the passage. The passage says that *mutual encouragement* (not hearing a pulpit sermon!) is the primary purpose of the church gathering. Mutual encouragement is a deterrent for willful sin. We ignore the full teaching of this passage to our own peril. Our spiritual prosperity is hinged upon corporate meetings that are marked by mutual (every-member) ministry.

Manifesting Jesus Christ in His Fullness

It is not without significance that the Greek word for church, *ekklesia*, literally means "assembly." This meshes nicely with the dominant thought in Paul's letters that the church is Christ in corporate expression (1 Cor. 12:1-27; Eph. 1:22-23; 4:1-16).

From man's perspective, the purpose of the church meeting is mutual edification. But from God's perspective, the purpose of the gathering is to express His Son. We gather together so that the Lord Jesus can manifest Himself in His fullness. When this happens, the Body is edified.

Note that the only way that Christ can be properly expressed is if *every* member freely supplies that aspect of the Lord that he or she has received. The Lord Jesus cannot fully disclose Himself through only one member. He is far too rich. In fact, His riches are inexhaustible (Eph. 3:8)!

So if the hand does not function in the gathering, Christ will not be manifested in fullness. Likewise, if the eyes fail to function, the Lord will be limited in revealing Himself. On the other hand, when every member of the Body functions in the meeting, Christ is seen. He is *Assembled* in our midst!

Consider the analogy of a puzzle. When each puzzle piece is properly positioned in relation to the other pieces, the puzzle is assembled. We see and understand the entire picture. So it is with Christ and His church.

God's desire of expressing His blessed Son to our hearts afresh is realized when every member of the *ekklesia* functions. It is realized when each believer supplies something of the Risen Head through the free-yet-orderly exercise of Spirit-endowed gifts. The highest purpose of the church meeting is to make the invisible Christ visible through His Body! We come together to reassemble the Lord Jesus Christ on earth!

Participatory meetings do not preclude the idea of planning. Nor do they suggest we should scrap all semblance of order and form. In 1 Corinthians 14, Paul formulates a number of broad guidelines designed to keep the meeting running in an orderly fashion.

In Paul's thought there is no tension between an *open* participatory meeting and an *orderly* one that edifies the saints. With scholarly insight, Robert Banks summarizes the texture of the early church gathering saying,

> *The Spirit's sovereignty over the gifts results in a stable, though not inflexible, distribution within the community and in their orderly, though not fixed, interplay in the gatherings . . . So then, provided certain basic principles of the Spirit's operation are kept in view: balance, intelligibility, evaluation, orderliness, and loving exercise, Paul sees no need to lay down any fixed rules for the community's proceedings . . . Paul therefore has no interest in constructing a fixed liturgy. This would restrict the freedom of God's communications. Each gathering of the community will have a structure, but it will emerge naturally from the particular combination of the gifts exercised. (Paul's Idea of Community)*

As far as content goes, the meetings were centered on Christ. Every word shared shed light on Him. Every song sang brought glory to Him. Every prayer offered brought Him into view. All the arrows of the meetings pointed to Him!

The early Christians did not meet to talk about theology. Nor did they have idle conversations about the Old Testament Scriptures. The early Christians had but one message in their meetings: It was Jesus Christ. As they experienced Him during their week, they came together to share Him with one another.

In essence, going to church in the first century meant *giving* more than *receiving*. You certainly did not attend the meeting to receive from a class of religious specialists called "the clergy!" You met to *serve* your brethren by ministering Christ. You sought to edify the church (Rom. 12:1-8; 1 Cor. 14:26; Heb. 10:24-25). And the Body was built up as a result.

The Question of Sustaining Force

In the typical institutional church, the religious machinery of the church "program" is the force that fuels and propels the church service. Consequently, if the Spirit of God were to leave an institutional church, His absence would go unnoticed.

The "business-as-usual" program would forge ahead. The worship would be unaffected. The liturgy (order of worship) would march on uninterrupted. The sermon would be preached; the doxology would be sung. Like Samson of old, the congregation would go right along with the religious program, "knowing not that the Lord had departed" (Judges 16:20).

By contrast, the only sustaining force of the early church gathering was the life of the Holy Spirit. The early Christians were liturgy-less, program-less, and ritual-less. They instead relied entirely upon the spiritual life of the individual members to maintain the church's existence and the quality of their gatherings.

If the life of the church was at a low ebb, everyone would notice it in the gathering. They couldn't overlook the cold chill of silence. What is more, if the Spirit of God left the meetings for good, the church would collapse altogether.

Stated simply, the first-century church knew no other sustaining influence other than the life of the Spirit. It did not rely on a man-programmed, humanly-planned, institutionally-fueled system to preserve its momentum.

The Mosaic tabernacle of old perfectly mirrors the modern institutional church. When God's presence left the holy tent, it became nothing more than a hollow shell accompanied by an impressive exterior. Tragically, even though the Lord's glory had departed, worshipers continued to offer their sacrifices at the empty tabernacle (1 Chron. 16:39-40; 2 Chron. 1:3-5; Jer. 7:12-14).

In the same way, the modern institutional church has confused the laying down of the altar with the consuming fire. Resting content with rearranging the pieces of the sacrifice upon the altar, the contemporary church no longer sees a need for the heavenly fire. (Except perhaps to make people feel good!)

The tragedy of the institutional church lies in its reliance upon a humanly-devised, program-driven religious system that serves to scaffold the "church" structure when the Spirit of God is absent. This moss-laden system betrays the fact that when the spontaneous life of the Spirit has ebbed away, it ceases to be the church in any Biblical sense—even though it may preserve the outward form. John W. Kennedy sums it up well:

> *Man always tries to conserve what God rejects, as church history adequately demonstrates. The result is seen in the bulk of present-day denominations, much of it a lifeless monument to glories that have long since disappeared . . . is it possible that God's people, in erecting 'lampstands' of bricks and mortar which have had to be kept up long after the light of the Spirit has gone out, have thwarted God's purpose? (The Secret of His Purpose)*

The Clerical Objection

While the NT envisions the early church meetings as open, participatory, and spontaneous, many modern clergymen refuse to approve of such meetings today. Modern clerical thinking on the subject goes something like this: "If I allowed *my* congregation to exercise its gifts in an open meeting, there would be sheer chaos. I have no choice but to control the services—lest the people spin out of control!"

Such an objection is severely flawed on several points. And it betrays a gross misunderstanding of God's ecclesiology. First, the notion that a clergyman has the authority to "allow" or "forbid" his fellow brethren to function in a meeting is built upon a skewed understanding of authority (see my book *Who is Your Covering?* for details). No human has the right to permit or prohibit the believing priesthood in the exercise of its Spirit-endowed gifts!

Second, the assumption that chaos would ensue if clerical control were removed betrays a lack of confidence in the Holy Spirit. It also reveals a lack of trust in God's people, something that violates the NT outlook (Rom. 15:14; 2 Cor. 2:3; 7:6; 8:22; Gal. 5:10; 2 Thess. 3:4; Phlm. 21; see also Heb. 6:9).

Third, the idea that the church meeting would turn into a tumultuous free-for-all is simply not true. If the saints are properly equipped on how to function under Christ's Headship, an open participatory meeting is a glorious event.

By the way, Christians do not become equipped by listening to sermons week after week while sitting muted in a pew. According to the first-century record, the saints are equipped by itinerant workers who teach them how to function. Such workers equip the saints, then they leave them on their own.

Granted, open participatory meetings may not always be as prim and proper as the traditional church service that runs flawlessly according to the pastor's (unwritten) liturgy.

Nevertheless, they reveal much more of the fullness of Christ than any human arrangement could manufacture.

There will be times that some may bring unprofitable ministry. This is particularly true in the infancy stages of a church's life. But the antidote is not to put a lid on spontaneous ministry. Those who overfunction and give unedifying ministry should be given instruction. At the beginning, this largely falls on the shoulders of those who are planting the church. (It will later shift to those who are older and more seasoned in the assembly.)

Recall what happened when Paul faced the frenzied morass in Corinth. (Corinth was a church that Paul planted.) Paul did not close the meeting. Nor did he introduce human officiation. Instead, he supplied the brethren with a number of broad guidelines to facilitate order and edification in the gatherings (1 Cor. 14:1ff.).

What is more, Paul was confident that the church would adhere to these guidelines. If similar guidelines are given and heeded today, there would be no need for human officiation, fixed liturgies, or heavily-scripted services. G.H. Lang explains,

> *And when they had gathered, no visible leader was in evidence, nor was a pre-arranged programme followed. Two or even three prophets might address the assembly; psalms, prayers, and other exercises were introduced spontaneously (1 Cor. 14). Great emphasis is laid on this as being the Divine intention by the fact that upon gross disorders arising, and the gatherings becoming unseemly and unprofitable (1 Cor. 11,14), the apostle by no means suggests any other form of service, but only lays down general principles, the application of which would prevent disorder and promote edification, the method of worship continuing essentially as before. There was indeed a duty to restrain vain and deceitful talking (1 Tim. 1:3; Titus 1:10-16); but there was no legislative or coercive power; the authority of the elders was purely moral . . . The*

Lord Himself, by His Spirit, was as really present as if He had been visible. Indeed, to faith He was visible; and He Himself being there, what servant could be so irreverent as to take out of His hands the control of the worship and ministry? But, on the other hand, most certainly it was not the case that anybody had liberty to minister. The liberty was for the Holy Spirit to do His will, not for His people to do as they willed . . . All rights in the house of God vest solely in the Son of God. The post-apostolic church quickly departed from this pattern. (The Churches of God)

At bottom, the tendency to reject the first-century styled church meeting unearths a lack of trust in the Holy Spirit. Rendle Short puts an even finer point on it saying,

We spoil God's workings, and we starve our souls, if we depart from this principle [open participatory meetings]. Someone may say, 'But will not things get into dreadful confusion if you seek to follow out these patterns? In those days they had the Holy Spirit to guide them, and shall not we go wildly astray, and have dull, confused, unprofitable, perhaps even unseemly meetings, unless we get someone to take charge?' Is that not practically a denial of the Holy Spirit? Do we dare deny that the Holy Spirit is still being given today? The Holy Spirit is at work today as much as He was at work in those days . . . Please do not think that what is sometimes called the 'open meeting' means that the saints are at the mercy of any unprofitable talker who thinks he has something to say, and would like to inflict himself upon them. The open meeting is not a meeting that is open to man. It is a meeting that is open to the Holy Spirit. There are some whose mouths must be stopped (Titus 1:10-14). Sometimes they may be stopped by prayer, and sometimes they have to be stopped by godly admonition . . . But because there is failure in carrying out the principle, do not let us give up on the principles of God. (The Churches of God)

In Numbers 11, we have the first appearance of clericalism in the Bible. Two servants of the Lord, Eldad and Medad, received God's Spirit and began to prophesy (vv. 26-27). In hasty response, a young zealot urged Moses to "restrain them" (v. 28). Moses reproved the young suppressor saying that *all* God's people should receive the Spirit and prophesy.

Moses' desire was fulfilled at Pentecost (Acts 2:17-18). And it continues to find fulfillment today (Acts 2:38-39; 1 Cor. 14:1,31). Unfortunately, the modern church does not lack for those who wish to again restrain Eldad and Medad from ministering in the Lord's house!

This world needs a multitude of believers who are of the spirit of Moses so that the Father would get what is rightfully His: A kingdom of functioning priests that serve under the Headship of His Son!

Headship vs. Lordship

The Bible draws a distinction between Headship and Lordship. Throughout the NT, the *Headship* of Christ virtually always has in view Christ's relationship with His Body (Eph. 1:22-23; 4:15; 5:23; Col. 1:18; 2:19). The *Lordship* of Christ virtually always has in view His relationship with individuals (Matt. 7:21-22; Luke 6:46; Acts 16:31; Rom. 10:9,13; 1 Cor. 6:17).

What Lordship is to the *individual*, Headship is to the *church*. Headship and Lordship are two dimensions of the same thing. Headship is Lordship worked out in the corporate life of God's people.

This distinction is important to grasp, for it throws light on the problem of church practice today. It is all too common for Christians to know Christ's Lordship and yet know nothing of His Headship.

A believer may truly submit to the Lordship of Jesus in his own personal life. He may obey what he understands in the Bible. He may pray fervently. He may live self-sacrificially. Yet at the same time, he may know nothing about shared ministry, mutual submission, or corporate testimony.

In the final analysis, to be subject to the Headship of Jesus means to respond to His will regarding the life and practice of the church. It includes such things as obtaining God's mind through mutual ministry and sharing. It includes obeying the Holy Spirit through mutual subjection and servanthood. It includes testifying to Jesus Christ collectively through mutual sharing and corporate witness.

Submission to the Headship of Christ incarnates the NT reality that Jesus is not only Lord of the *lives of men.* He is also Master of the *life of the church.* Shockingly, Scripture is plain that when Christ's Headship is established and given concrete expression in the earth, He will become Head over all things in the universe (Col. 1:16-18).

With stirring clarity, Arthur Wallis describes the inseparable connection between Christ's Headship and His Lordship saying,

> *Christ taught that our commitment to Him must be wholehearted. It means denying oneself, taking up the cross and following Him. But Scripture is equally clear that our attitude toward Christ is reflected in our attitude toward His people. As is our attitude toward the Head, so will our attitude be to His Body. You cannot be wholehearted toward Christ but only halfhearted toward His church. (The Radical Christian)*

Final Thoughts

I end this chapter with several questions for thought:

Is it possible that modern evangelicalism has held the doctrine of the believing priesthood only *intellectually,* but has failed to *practically* apply it due to the subtle entrapment of deeply entrenched traditions? Do our modern church services, largely built around the sermon of one man and the worship program of an established team, reflect the normative gatherings that we find in our Bibles? Or are they at odds with it? Why would open participatory meetings be good for the early Christians, but somehow be unworkable for us today? Finally, is our practice of the church an expression of the complete Headship of Jesus Christ or the headship of man?

If you are honest with yourself, you will quickly discover that the modern church has strayed far afield from its original purpose.

CHAPTER 2

THE FELLOWSHIP MEAL

The NT clearly demonstrates that mutual edification was the primary purpose of the early church gathering. But it equally shows that the practice of "breaking bread," or the Lord's Supper, was one of its central features. The regular practice of the church of Troas and the church of Corinth indicate this:

And upon the first day of the week, when the disciples CAME TOGETHER TO BREAK BREAD, Paul preached. (Acts 20:7)

WHEN YOU COME TOGETHER IN THE SAME PLACE IT IS NOT TO EAT THE LORD'S SUPPER, for in eating every one taketh before the other his own supper: and one is hungry, and another is drunken . . . So then, my brothers, when you COME TOGETHER TO EAT wait for one another. (1 Cor. 11:20-21,33)

And they [the saints in Jerusalem] CONTINUED STEDFASTLY in the apostles' doctrine and fellowship, in THE BREAKING OF BREAD, and in prayers. (Acts 2:42)

The Lord's Supper held a special place in the gatherings of the early church. We are told that the church in Troas came together to break bread every Lord's day. In 1 Corinthians, Paul chided the Corinthians for not coming together to eat the Lord's Supper (which they should have). But for coming together to eat their own! Further, the church in Jerusalem continued steadfastly in observing the Lord's Supper.

Broken Bread

Why did the breaking of bread have such a significant place in the early church? It is because it embodies the major features of the Christian life.

First, the broken bread points us to the humanity of Jesus. The Son of glory took upon Himself the form of a servant. He lowered Himself by becoming a man.

Similarly, the bread—being the most basic and lowly of all foods—points to the humility of our Lord. By taking on our humanity, Jesus has become accessible to all—just as bread is available to every one, both rich and poor.

The breaking of bread reminds us of the cross upon which our Lord's Body was broken. Bread is made from the crushed wheat. Wine is made from the pressed grape. Both elements represent death.

The breaking of bread not only depicts the death of Christ, it also shows forth His resurrection. The grain of wheat has gone into the ground. Yet it now lives to produce many grains like itself (John 12:24). Thus if we eat Christ's flesh and drink His Blood, we obtain His life (John 6:53). This is resurrection—life out of death.

The revelation of the Risen Christ is also bound up with the bread. When the Risen Lord ate with His disciples, it was bread that He broke with them (John 21:13). In like manner, the Resurrected Christ appeared to the two men on the Emmaus road. However, their eyes were not opened to recognize Him until He had broken and distributed the bread (Luke 24:30-32).

The testimony of the oneness of Christ's Body is also embodied in the breaking of bread. Recall that there was only one loaf that the early Christians broke. Paul writes, "Because there is *one* loaf, we, who are many, are *one* Body, for we all partake of the *one* loaf" (1 Cor. 10:17).

Surely the Lord is grieved when multitudes of His children living in the same locale break bread as though they were each a separate Body. To break bread while having a sectarian spirit is a serious thing in the sight of God. This was the error of Corinth. And Paul chided them sternly for it (1 Cor. 11:27-29).

A Covenant Meal

The early church took the Lord's Supper in the context of a normal meal. When the Master Himself instituted the Supper, it was taken as part of the Passover feast (Luke 22:15-20). In fact, the Passover was the forerunner of the Lord's Supper.

The whole of 1 Corinthians 11 makes clear that the believers gathered to eat the Supper as a meal. One would find himself hard-pressed to get drunk on a thimble of grape juice or satisfy his hunger with a bite-sized cracker (vv. 21-22; 33-34)!

Further, the NT word for "supper" literally means a dinner, a meal, or a banquet. And the Greek word for "table" indicates a table in which a full, square meal is spread (Luke 22:14; 1 Cor. 10:21).

Consequently, the Lord's Supper of the early church comprised a fellowship meal. (Today, NT scholars from all denominational persuasions agree on this.) It was the table communion of the saints. A family festival. A covenant meal. For this reason the early church referred to the Supper as the *Agape,* or love feast (2 Pet. 2:13; Jude 12).

Regrettably, centuries of ecclesiastical tradition have made today's truncated version of the Supper something far removed from what it was in the first century. As a result, the communal meaning of the breaking of bread has been largely lost. It is no longer the Lord's Supper. Today it would better be called the Savior's Sampler, the Nazarene Niblet, or the Lord's Appetizer! I am sorry, but we can hardly call a cracker crumb and a shotglass of juice a supper!

Robert Banks observes the following regarding the Lord's Supper as a meal:

The most visible and profound way in which the community gives physical expression to its fellowship is the common meal. The word 'deipnon' (1 Cor. 11:20), meaning 'dinner,' tells us that it was not a token meal (as it has become since) or part of a meal (as it is sometimes envisaged), but an entire, ordinary meal . . . Paul's injunctions to the 'hungry' to eat before they leave home (vv. 22,34) do not represent the beginnings of a separation of the Lord's Supper from the meal itself. He is merely trying to avoid abuses that had entered into the meal at Corinth . . . This meal is vital, for as the members of the community eat and drink together their unity comes to visible expression. The meal is therefore a truly social event . . . the meal that they shared together reminded the members of their relationship with Christ and one another and deepened those relationships in the same way that participation in an ordinary meal cements and symbolizes the bond between a family or group. (Paul's Idea of Community)

G.H. Lang argues along the same lines saying,

It was during the social meal connected with the Passover feast that the Lord had introduced the new association of that bread and cup with His own Person and work. Likewise does 1 Cor. 11 show that the believers at Corinth observed the Supper in connexion with a social meal of the whole company. This was known as the 'Agape' or feast of love, and though it had led to abuses at Corinth the apostle does not repudiate the practice but regulates its observance . . . It is healthful that this picture rise before the mind. An ordinary house the place; a customary meal the occasion; the Supper quietly and easily conjoined therewith. No ecclesiastical building, no priest or functionary, no altar or sacrifice, no vestments or ornaments, as lights, incense, crucifixes, no formality. The Supper observed in simplicity; the home dignified thereby, the ordinary meal sanctified and solemnized. (The Churches of God)

The Wedding Feast to Come

The breaking of bread also points to Christ's future coming in glory. Then, the Bridegroom will preside at that sumptuous wedding feast to sup with His beloved Bride in His Father's kingdom (Matt. 26:29). The Lord's Supper, therefore, possesses eschatological overtones. It is a last-days feast. A figure of the Messianic Banquet that will occur at His future coming (Matt. 22:1-14; 26:29; Luke 12:35-38; 15:22-32; Rev. 19:9).

The Lord's supper is not a morbid reminder of Christ's sufferings. Nor is it an occasion where we mourn over our sins. No! The Supper is a cheerful reminder of who Jesus Christ is. It reminds us of His glorious victory at Calvary. And it reminds us of His coming kingdom.

The Lord's Supper, therefore, is a celebration. It is a happy, conversational meal. It is a banquet of joy marked by sharing and thanksgiving (Luke 22:17; Acts 2:46; 1 Cor. 10:16). It is a foretaste of the wedding feast that is to come. Beyond this, it is the Bride's visible petition for her Bridegroom to return for her.

The Supper Transcends Time

In sum, the breaking of bread possesses past, present, and future implications. It is a re-proclamation of the Lord's sacrificial death for us in the *past*. It is a re-declaration of His ever abiding nearness with us in the *present*. And it is a re-pronouncement of the hope of His coming in the *future*.

The Lord's Supper also witnesses to the three chief virtues: faith, hope, and love. Through the Supper, we re-ground ourselves in that glorious salvation that is ours by *faith*. We re-express our *love* for the brethren as we reflect on the one Body.

And we rejoice in the *hope* of our Lord's soon return. By observing the Supper correctly, we "proclaim (present) the Lord's death (past) till He comes (future)."

Catholics have made the Lord's Supper literal and sacrificial. Every time they take the Eucharist, they believe that Christ is being re-sacrificed for our sins. Protestants have made the Supper merely symbolic and commemorative. They believe it is merely a reminder of the cross.

But the Lord's Supper is neither a perpetual sacrifice (the Catholic view) nor an empty ritual (the Protestant practice). It carries no sacramental overtones. Nor can it be properly conceived as simply a memorial.

The Lord's Supper is a *spiritual reality*. The Holy Spirit is present in it. Through the Supper, the Spirit reveals the living Christ to the hearts of His beloved saints. In the Supper, we sup with Him through the one loaf and the one cup.

Our Lord often used the imagery of eating and drinking to depict our spiritual communion with Him (John 4:14; 6:51; 7:37; Rev. 3:20). Eric Svendsen aptly summarizes the chief features of the Lord's Supper:

> *The Supper held a wide range of purposes. First, it served as an expression of concern for the poor in the believing community. In all likelihood, the Supper was a potluck of sorts provided by the rich to show their love for less fortunate Christians. It is probably this purpose that resulted in the adoption of the title 'Agape.' A second dimension of the Supper is that it compelled the Christian community to live out the theology of equality of status in Christ, violating the Hellenistic societal norm to hold homogenous banquets where class distinctions were acutely recognized . . . Another very important, yet oft-missed focus of the Supper is its eschatological focus. The Lord's Supper prefigures the Messianic Banquet and acts as a means to petition Messiah to come again. The Supper*

*is to be repeated on a regular basis in order to sound
this petition and to give the participants the
opportunity to proclaim with one voice, 'Maranatha!'
(The Table of the Lord)*

The Supper and the Table

The NT makes a careful distinction between the Lord's
Supper and the Lord's *Table*. Both terms point to the single
practice of breaking bread. But there is a subtle difference in
emphasis.

In 1 Corinthians 10:16-22, Paul speaks about the Lord's
Table (v. 21). There the emphasis is on the church. The bread
points to the unified Body of Christ (v. 17). *Communion* and
oneness are the dominant thoughts in the Table.

The Pharisees had a closed, elitist table of fellowship. But
the Lord's Table is all-inclusive. Jesus opens it to all who wish
to sup with Him (Luke 6:27-32; 7:36-50; 11:37-52; 15:1-2;
19:1-9). Therefore, the Table sharpens our focus on the
unrestricted communion that Christ has with His people—and
all who name His name (1 Cor. 10:16-17).

In 1 Corinthians 11:17-34, Paul speaks about the Lord's
Supper (v. 20). There the emphasis is on the death of the Lord
Jesus for us. The bread points to the physical Body of our Lord
that was slain for our redemption (v. 24).

Remembering and *proclaiming* are the principal thoughts
in the Supper. They direct our attention to remember Jesus
Christ and to declare His sacrificial-death (vv. 25-26).

In the Table, it is the horizontal relationship of the believing community that is in view. In the Supper, it is the
vertical relationship between the believers and Christ that is in
view.

Put differently, the Table is the place of fellowship,
sharing, and eating. The Supper is the essence of the meal. The
Table is the *environment* for our communion. The Supper is
the *substance* of our communion. While the Table and the

Supper are distinct, they are not separate. They are but two sides to the same coin.

The Centrality of the Supper

From a practical standpoint, the rightful place of the Lord's Supper in the church meeting delivers us from our natural penchant to be self-absorbed. When our meetings climax around His Table, all attention is taken off ourselves. It is instead fastened upon Christ.

The breaking of bread reminds us of the centrality of the invisible Head who is always present when we gather. Perhaps this is why the Table of the Lord is the only material thing that Scripture mentions as being present in the meeting of the church. The words of Hugh Kane are fitting:

That which occupied the most conspicuous place in the assemblies of God's people was neither a 'preacher' nor a 'pulpit' but a 'table' on which rested the symbols, 'bread and wine.' Those early believers were gathered unto Him (Matt. 18:20). He was the magnet to which their hearts were drawn and by which they were charmed and satisfied.. The beauty of that method of gathering was its very simplicity. No arrangements nor adornments of men! No 'altar service,' no 'priestly vestments,' no specially 'robed choirs' . . . they had no one to lead their assembly worship but the Holy Spirit; He was sufficient. He directed their hearts to Christ . . . it was beautiful and God-honoring because it was His own arrangement. The vainglory of the flesh found no place there. No one was seen but 'Jesus only.' (My Reasons)

These are but a few precious truths bound up with the breaking of bread. And they help explain why the early Christians made it a central part of their gatherings. Suffice it to say that the Lord Jesus Himself instituted the Supper (Matt. 26:26). His apostles then handed it down to us (1 Cor. 11:2).

With this in view, should not NT teaching and example shape our approach to the Lord's Supper today? The Lord help us to no longer neglect the unique place that God has reserved for His Son's Table in our midst.

CHAPTER 3

THE CHURCH IN THE HOUSE

S*o where do you go to church?* This question is commonplace today. Yet the question itself touches a significant note in God's purpose.

Suppose that a new employee was recently hired at your workplace. You learn that he is a Christian. Upon asking what church he attends, he responds by saying: "I attend a church that meets in a home."

Now what are the thoughts that run through your mind? Do you think, "Well, that's rather strange. This guy must be a religious misfit of some sort." Or, "He's probably part of some cult or flaky fringe group." Or, "There must be something wrong with him. If there wasn't, he would be going to a *regular* church?" Or, "This guy certainly must be a rebel of some sort. He's probably a loose canon on the deck—unable to submit to authority. Else he would be attending a *normal* church—you know, the kind that meets in a building!"

Unfortunately, these are the thoughts that run through the minds of many modern Christians whenever the idea of a "house church" is brought to their attention. But here is the punch line. That new employee's place of meeting is identical to that of *every* Christian mentioned in the NT!

In fact, the church of Jesus Christ met in the homes of its members for the first three hundred years after its birth! NT scholar Robert Banks remarks,

Whether we are considering the smaller gatherings of only some Christians in a city or the larger meetings involving the whole Christian population, it is in the home of one of the members that 'ekklesia' is held—for example in the

'upper room.' Not until the third century do we have evidence of special buildings being constructed for Christian gatherings. (Paul's Idea of Community)

The Witness of the Early Christians

The common meeting place for the early Christians was none other than the home. Anything else would have been the exception. And the early believers would have looked upon it as being *out of* the ordinary. Note the following passages:

. . . And [the believers went about] breaking bread from HOUSE TO HOUSE . . . (Acts 2:46)

As for Saul, he made havock of the CHURCH, entering into every HOUSE . . . (Acts 8:3)

. . . I did not shrink from declaring to you anything that was profitable, teaching you publicly and from HOUSE TO HOUSE . . . (Acts 20:20, NASB)

Greet Priscilla and Aquila my helpers in Christ Jesus . . . Likewise greet the CHURCH that is in their HOUSE . . . (Rom. 16:3,5)

The churches of Asia salute you. Aquila and Priscilla salute you much in the Lord, with the CHURCH that is in their HOUSE. (1 Cor. 16:19)

Salute the brethren which are in Laodicea, and Nymphas, and the CHURCH which is in his HOUSE. (Col. 4:15)

And to our beloved Apphia, and Archippus our fellowsoldier, and to the CHURCH in thy HOUSE. (Phlm. 2)

If there come any unto you, and bring not this doctrine, receive him not into the HOUSE, neither bid him God speed. (2 John 10)

The above Scriptures amply demonstrate that the early church had its meetings in the hospitable homes of its members (see also Acts 2:2; 9:11; 10:32; 12:12; 16:15,34,40; 17:5; 18:7; 21:8).

The first-century believers knew nothing of what would correspond to the "church" edifice of today. Neither did they know anything about houses converted into basilicas. That is, none of them had hardwood pews bolted to the floor and a pulpit accompanying the living room furniture! While such oddities exist in the 20th century, they were foreign to the first Christians.

The early believers assembled together in simple, ordinary, livable houses. They knew nothing of "church-houses." They only knew the "church in the house."

What did the church do when it grew too large to assemble in a single house? It certainly did not erect a building. It simply multiplied and met in several other homes following the "house to house principle" (Acts 2:46; 20:20).

Modern scholarship agrees that the early church was essentially a network of home-based meetings. So if there is such a thing as a *normal* church, it is the church that meets in the house! Or as one writer put it, "If there is a NT form of the church, it is the house church."

Notwithstanding, some have tried to argue that the primitive Christians would have erected specialized buildings if they were not under persecution. They say that the Christians met in homes to hide from their persecutors. While this idea is popular, it is rooted in pure conjecture. It also maps poorly to the historical evidence. Bill Grimes crystallizes the point saying,

Many dismiss early house churches as the result of per-secution. However, any church history textbook will reveal that persecution prior to A.D. 250 was sporadic, localized and usually the result of mob hostility rather than a decree of a Roman official. This 'persecution' myth also clashes with Scripture. Acts 2:46-47 describes home meetings at a time when the church was 'enjoying the favor of all the people.' When persecution did break out, meeting in homes didn't stop Saul from knowing just where to go to arrest believers (Acts 8:3). They obviously made no secret about where they met. (Toward a House Church Theology)

If we read the NT with an eye for understanding how the first-century Christians related to one another, we shall quickly discover why they met in homes. The reasons are in harmony with spiritual principle. So they apply to us today with equal force. Let us explore some of them now.

(1) The Home Testifies that the People Comprise God's House

The contemporary notion of "church" is frequently associated with a building. (It is commonly called "the sanctuary" or "the house of God.") According to the Bible, however, it is the *believers* indwelt with God's life that are named the church! The saints are called "the house of God"—never the bricks and the mortar.

In Judaism the temple is the sanctified meeting place. In Christianity the believing community is the temple. In this way, the spatial location of the early Christian gathering cut directly against the religious customs of the first century.

Both Judaism and paganism teach that there must be a sanctified place for Divine worship. Consequently, the Jews erected special buildings for their corporate worship (syn-agogues). So did the pagans (shrines). Not so with Christianity.

The early believers understood that God sanctifies people, not objects.

Interestingly, the early church was the only religious group in the first century that met exclusively in homes. It would have been quite natural for them to pursue their Jewish heritage and erect buildings to suit their needs. But they intentionally kept from doing so.

Perhaps the early believers knew the confusion that sanctified buildings would produce. Hence, they kept from erecting them to preserve the testimony that *the people* comprised the living stones of God's habitation.

(2) The Home is the Natural Setting for One-Anothering

The apostolic instructions concerning the church meeting are best suited for a small group setting like the home. Christian principles like mutual participation (Heb. 10:24-25); the exercise of spiritual gifts (1 Cor. 14:26); the building together of the brethren into an intentional, face-to-face community (Eph. 2:21-22); the communal meal (1 Cor. 11); the open transparency and mutual submission of members one toward another (Rom. 15:14; Gal. 6:1-2; Jas. 5:16,19-20); the freedom for interactive dialogue (1 Cor. 14:29-40); and the liberty-oriented *koinonia* (shared life) of the Holy Spirit (2 Cor. 3:17; 13:14) all operate best in a small group setting like the home.

In sum, the fifty-eight "one-another" exhortations in the NT can only be fleshed out in a house-like environment. For this reason, the home church meeting is highly conducive to the realization of God's eternal purpose. A purpose that is centered upon the "building together" of the Body into the Head (Eph. 2:19-22).

(3) The Home Represents the Simplicity of Christ

The home represents humility, naturalness, and pure simplicity—the outstanding marks of the early church (Acts 2:46;
2 Cor. 11:3). The house is a far more humble place than the
stately religious edifices of our day with their lofty steeples
and elegant decor. In this way, most modern "church"
buildings reflect the boastings of this world rather than the
meek and lowly Savior whose name we bear.

What is more, the overhead costs of a religious building
costs the brethren much financial loss. How much freer their
hands would be to support apostolic workers ("church plant-
ers") and help the poor among them if they did not have to
bear such a heavy burden.

(4) The Home Reflects the Family Nature of the Church

There is a natural affinity between the home meeting and
the family theme of the church that saturates Paul's writings.
Because the home is the native environment of the family, it
naturally furnishes the *ekklesia* with a familial atmosphere.
The very atmosphere that pervaded the life of the early
Christians.

In stark contrast, the artificial environment of the church
building promotes an impersonal climate that inhibits intimacy and participation. The conventional "church" edifice
produces a certain stuffiness. The rigid formalism of the
building runs contrary to the refreshing, unofficial air that the
home meeting breathes.

Further, it is easy to "get lost" in a large building. Because
of the spacious and remote nature of the basilica church, it is
easy for folks to go unnoticed. Or worse, to hide in their sins.
Not so in a home. All our warts show there. And rightly so.
Everyone in the gathering is known, accepted, and encouraged.

In addition, the formal manner in which things are done in the basilica church tends to discourage the mutual intercourse and spontaneity that characterized the early Christian gatherings. Exegete the architecture of a typical church building and you will discover that it effectively teaches the church to be passive.

The interior structure of the building is not designed for interpersonal communication, mutual ministry, or spiritual fellowship. Instead, it is designed for a rigid one-way communication—pulpit to pew, leader to congregation.

The typical "church" edifice is strikingly similar to a lecture hall or cinema. The congregation is carefully arranged in pews (or chairs) to see and hear the pastor (or priest) speak from the pulpit. The people are focused on a single point—the clergy leader and his pulpit. (In liturgical churches, the table/altar takes the place of the pulpit as the central point of reference. But in both cases, the building promotes a clergy centrality.)

Moreover, the place where the pastor and staff are seated is normally elevated above the seating of the congregation. Such an arrangement reinforces the unbiblical clergy/laity chasm. It also feeds the spectator-mentality that afflicts most of the Body of Christ today. W.J. Pethybridge astutely observes,

In a small group meeting in the friendly associations of a home, everybody can know each other and relationships are more real and less formal. With the smaller number it is possible for everybody to take an active part in the meeting, and so the whole Body of Christ present can function . . . Having a special building for meetings nearly always involves the idea of a special person as minister developing into 'one man ministry' and preventing the full exercise of the priesthood of all believers. (The Lost Secret of the Early Church)

The early Christians conducted their meetings in the home to express the character of church life. They met in houses to encourage the family dimension of their worship, fellowship, and ministry.

The meetings in the home naturally made the saints feel that the church's interests were their interests. It fostered a sense of closeness between themselves and the church, rather than distancing them from it. By contrast, most modern Christians attend "church" as remote spectators. Not as active participants.

In short, the house church meeting provided both the connectedness and deep-seated relationships that characterizes the *ekklesia*. The spirit of the home-based meeting furnished the saints with a family-like atmosphere where true fellowship occurred shoulder-to-shoulder, face-to-face, and eyeball-to-eyeball.

The home meeting provided a climate that fostered open communication, spiritual cohesiveness, and unreserved communion. These are necessary features for the full flourishing of the *koinonia* (shared fellowship) of the Holy Spirit.

In all of these ways, the house church meeting is fundamentally Biblical. It is also spiritually practical. And it is strikingly at odds with the modern pulpit-pew styled service where believers are forced to fellowship with the back of someone's head for an hour or two! Watchman Nee sums it up nicely saying,

In our assemblies today we must return to the principle of the 'upper room.' The ground floor is a place for business, a place for men to come and go; but there is more of a home atmosphere about the upper room, and the gatherings of God's children are family affairs. The Last Supper was in an upper room, so was Pentecost, and so again was the meeting [in Troas]. God wants the intimacy of the 'upper room' to mark the gatherings of His children, not the stiff formality of an imposing public edifice. That is why in the Word of God we find His children meeting in the family atmosphere of a private home . . . we should try and encourage meetings in the homes of the Christians . .

the homes of the brethren will nearly always meet the needs of the church meetings. (The Normal Christian Church Life)

(5) The Home Models Spiritual Authenticity

We live in a day where many, especially youth, are searching for spiritual authenticity. To these seekers, churches that meet in amphitheaters, crystal cathedrals, and ivory-towered domes appear superficial and shallow.

By contrast, the church in the home serves as a fruitful testimony of spiritual reality. For many, the house church is a refreshing witness against those religious institutions that equate glamourous buildings and multimillion dollar budgets with success.

Equally so, many unbelievers will not attend a modern religious service held in a basilica church where they are expected to "dress up" for the show. Yet they feel unthreatened and uninhibited gathering in the natural comfort of someone's house. There they can be themselves.

The unprofessional atmosphere of the home, as opposed to a clinical building, is much more inviting. Perhaps this is another reason why the early Christians chose to gather in homes rather than erecting shrines, sanctuaries, and synagogues as did the other religions of their day.

Ironically, many modern Christians believe that if a church does not own a building, its testimony to the world is inhibited and its growth stifled. But nothing could be further from the truth. Howard Snyder observes,

. . . Whatever else buildings are good for, they are not essential either for numerical growth or spiritual depth. The early church possessed both these qualities, and the church's greatest period of vitality and growth until recent times was during the first two centuries A.D. In other words, the church grew fastest when it did not have the help—or hindrance—of church buildings. (The Problem of Wineskins, used by permission of the author)

The Social Location of the Church

What has been said thus far can be reduced to this simple yet profound observation: The social location of the church meeting both expresses and influences the character of the church itself!

Put another way, the spatial setting of the church possesses theological significance. In the typical "sanctuary" or "chapel," the pulpit, the pews (or rowed chairs) and the massified space breathe a formal air that inhibits interaction and relatedness.

The peculiar features of a home produce the opposite effects. The low-volume seating. The casual atmosphere. The convivial setting for shared meals. The personalized space of soft sofas. All these characteristics contain a relational subtext that befits mutual ministry.

Stated simply, the early church met in the homes of its members for spiritually viable reasons. The modern basilica church undermines those reasons! Howard Snyder astutely remarks,

House churches have probably been the most common form of Christian social organization in all church history . . . Despite what we might think if we simply look around us here, hundreds of thousands of Christian house churches exist today in North America, South America, Europe, China, Australia, Eastern Europe, and in many other

*places around the world. In some sense, they are the un-
derground church, and as such, represent the hidden
stream of church history. But although they are hidden,
and in most places not the culturally dominant form, these
house churches probably represent the largest number of
Christians worldwide . . . The NT teaches us that the
church is a community in which all are gifted and all have
ministry. The church as taught in Scripture is a new social
reality that models and incarnates the respect and concern
for people that we see in Jesus Himself. This is our high
calling. And yet the church, in fact, often betrays this
calling. House churches are a big part of the way out of
this betrayal and this paradox. Face-to-face community
breeds mutual respect, mutual responsibility, mutual
submission, and mutual ministry. The sociology of the
house church fosters a sense of equality and mutual worth,
though it doesn't guarantee it as the Corinthian church
shows . . . In the house church model, equality and mutual
ministry are not the result of some program or educational
process; they are inherent in the very forms of the church
itself. Because in the house church everyone is valued and
known—everyone has a place by definition. The house
church provides an environment of mutual care and
encouragement that tends to foster a wide range of gifts
and ministries. The NT principles of the priesthood of
believers, the gifts of the Spirit, and mutual ministry are
found most naturally in this informal context . . . House
churches are revolutionary because they incarnate this
radical teaching that all are gifted and all are ministers.
They offer some hope for healing the Body of Christ from
some of its worst heresies: that some believers are more
valuable than others, that only some Christians are
ministers, and that the gifts of the Spirit are no longer to
function in our age. These heresies cannot be healed in
theory or in theology only. They must be healed in practice*

*and relationship in the social form of the church. (Taken
from a lecture entitled "Why House Churches Today?,"
presented at Fuller Theological Seminary, Feb. 24, 1996.
Used by permission of the author)*

Two Kinds of Meetings

That the normative meeting place for the early church was
the home is beyond dispute. But does this suggest that it is
never appropriate for a church to gather in any other location?
No, it does not.

On special occasions when it was necessary for "the whole
church" to gather together, the church in Jerusalem met in large
settings such as the open courts of the temple and Solomon's
porch (Acts 2:46a; 5:12).

But such large group gatherings did not rival the normative
location for the regular church meeting, which was the house
(Acts 2:46b). Nor did it set a Biblical precedent for Christians
to *erect* their own buildings. The temple courts and Solomon's
portico were public, outdoor arenas that were already in
existence *before* the first Christians appeared. These large
group settings simply accommodated the "whole church" when
it was necessary to bring it together for a particular purpose.

In the beginning days of the church's existence, the
apostles used such locations to hold special ministry meetings
for the vast number of believers and unbelievers in Jerusalem
(Acts 3:11-26; 5:20-21,25,42).

Instances where we find the apostles going to the synagogues should not be confused with church meetings. These
were *evangelistic* meetings designed to preach the gospel to
unsaved Jews. Again, the church meeting is primarily for the
edification of believers. The evangelistic meeting is primarily
for the salvation of unbelievers.

Perhaps the Holy Spirit has led and will lead some to
assemble in a building from time to time. But the Spirit will

only do so if it truly suits the *Lord's* purposes. And let it be clear that if God leads a church in this direction, it will not be driven by human zeal, energy, and advertising machinery—and then cloaked over with religious talk justifying the decision!

Consequently, we must guard against the fleshly tendency to practice something simply because it represents the latest spiritual fad of the day. The Lord spare us from falling into the peril of ancient Israel wherein they aimlessly "followed after the nations."

Notwithstanding, is there not something monumental for us to glean from the apostolic practice of meeting in homes? Should not *house church* meetings be more the rule than the exception due to the benefits that are bound up with them?

If nothing else, should we not repent of our fleshly criticism and unjustified fear of those churches that meet exclusively in homes—invalidly dooming them to sub-normal status? May we be delivered from mindlessly adopting the present *edifice complex* because it is the conventional thing to do!

Upon examining the Biblical evidence, the question in our minds regarding the location of the church meeting ought not to be, "Why do some meet in homes." It rather should be, "Why is it that so many *do not* meet in homes!?"

CHAPTER 4

THE CHURCH AS FAMILY

Scripture is undeniably clear that all who possess the indwelling life of the Risen Head make up the church. The natural implication of this glorious truth is that the church is *a family*. A family whose members are joined together, organically connected, and inseparably related by Divine life.

This being the case, one cannot *join* the church. If you are in Christ Jesus, you are joined already! You are joined by birth (the new birth).

Our limbs are joined to our physical bodies by life, and not by organization, invitation, creedal confession, or catechism. So too, we are joined to Jesus Christ and His Body simply by *life*. If you are a believer in Christ then you share one new life with all other reborn believers. In becoming a Christian, you have become part of a new family. And that family is the *ekklesia*—the habitat of God's people.

It is for this reason that the NT frequently refers to the church as "the household," or "family," of God (Gal. 6:10; Eph. 2:19; 1 Tim. 3:15; Heb. 3:6; 10:21; 1 Pet. 2:5). The NT authors describe the church with a variety of different images—such as a body, a bride, a nation, a priesthood, and an army. But their favorite metaphor is *the family*.

Familial terms like "new birth," "children of God," "sons of God," brethren," "fathers," "sisters," "brothers," and "household" are punctuated throughout the NT documents.

Doubtlessly, most Christians have no trouble giving glib assent to the idea that the church is a family. Yet there is a vast difference between giving mere mental assent to the family nature of the church and in fleshing out its sober implications. Regrettably, many modern Christians give mere lip-service to the fact that their fellow brethren are their brothers and sisters. Few live as though this were the case.

Family Life

In understanding the church to be the family of God, let us first wrestle with the challenging question of how a family is to live. A normal family lives under the same roof, does it not? The members of a healthy family take care of, spend time with, admonish, encourage, serve, and look after one another.

Families typically eat together. They greet one another with affection. They squabble. They reconcile. They protect one another. And they help each other in a pinch. The early church embodied all of these family norms (Acts 2:46; Rom. 12:10,13,16; 1 Cor. 16:20; 2 Cor. 13:12; Gal. 5:13; 1 Thess. 5:26; 1 Pet. 5:14).

Is this not the picture that is before us throughout the book of Acts? Luke tells us that the early believers "were together and had everything in common" (2:44, NIV)."Every day they continued to meet together" (2:46, NIV). "All the believers were one in heart and mind. No one claimed that any of his possessions were his own, but they shared everything they had" (4:32, NIV). And why? Because the church is a family.

The sense of family and community was so high among the early believers that it has been said that the Christian network of care in the first century was the third strongest influence in the Roman empire! If you were a Christian in the first century, you did not need insurance. The church was your insurance!

The brethren were Divinely called to bear the burdens of the believing community (Rom. 12:13; Gal. 6:2,9-10; Heb. 13:16; 1 John 3:17-18). And they did (Acts 6:1-7; 1 Tim. 5:2-16; Heb. 6:10). And why? Because the church is a family.

In the early church, new converts were received with open arms. They were not ignored or treated with irrational suspicion. The interests of the church were shared by each individual member (Phil. 2:4). The physical and spiritual children in the church were viewed as belonging to the church.

The early Christians looked after one another. They took responsibility for each other. They saw themselves as a shared-life community—an extended household of brothers and sisters, fathers and mothers (Mark 10:29-30). And why? Because the church is a family.

Most Americans do not hesitate to help their blood kin when they meet financial hardships. Yet how many modern Christians react in the same way when their brother or sister in Christ has a financial crisis? Do you feel a sense of familial obligation to help such ones? Or do you feel detached from their situation? Such a disturbing question sorely tests our alleged belief that the church is indeed a family.

It is sobering to note that the early Christians were not forced to look to secular government for financial assistance. Instead, they took responsibility for those who had lack (2 Cor. 8:12-15; Rom. 12:13). They regarded each member as "their own." They saw themselves as "members one of another" (Eph. 4:25).

This being so, the early Christians operated on the principle of mutual care. Paul put it this way: "He that had gathered much had nothing left over; and he that had gathered little had no lack." And why? Because the church is a family.

In the NT church, the brethren appreciated one another. Relationships were paramount. Putting it in the context of modern times, if you had fellowship with a group of believers in one city and then moved to another at a later time, the first group would not cut off relations with you. And why? Because the church is a family.

Moreover, the *whole* Body is a family and not a particular section of it. When our blood relatives move away, do we stop relating to them simply because they are out of sight? How much stronger are the ties of Divine life than human blood!?

Community or Corporation?

Significantly, the NT writers never use the imagery of a business corporation to depict the church. Unlike the institutional church, the early Christians knew nothing of spending colossal figures on building programs and projects at the expense of bearing the burdens of their fellow brethren.

Many contemporary churches have essentially become nothing more than high-powered enterprises that bear more resemblance to General Motors than to the apostolic community! With masterful eloquence, Hal Miller writes,

> *Unfortunately, the metaphor that dominates most of American Christianity doesn't help us much; we usually envision the church as a corporation. The pastor is the CEO, there are committees and boards. Evangelism is the manufacturing process by which we make our product, and sales can be charted, compared, and forecast. Of course, this manufacturing process goes on in a growth economy so that any corporation-church whose annual sales figures aren't up from last year's is in trouble. Americans are quite single-minded in their captivity to the corporation metaphor. And it isn't even Biblical. ("Church as Body, Church as Family," Voices in the Wilderness, May/June '89)*

Regrettably, many Christians today have succumbed to the intoxicating seductions of an individualistic, materialistic, business-oriented, consumer-driven, self-serving society. By contrast, the NT church did not commit itself to a "bigger-is-better," "business-as-usual" mentality.

It knew nothing of a paid professional staff that held the other brethren at arm's distance—only "letting their hair down" with other professionals in the same profession! Neither did it know anything about a separate caste-system where those elevated into positions of official authority looked down upon their fellow brethren through the artificial lens of clerical glasses.

Instead, the leaders of the NT church saw themselves as mere brethren. Members of the same family. Having no designations that tended toward separation. Each member, including every leader, was easily accessible to the other members.

The spirit of community, personal relationship, and bonding was chief among all the early believers. They were intimate. They were interdependent. And they were ever growing together into the Head. In this way, the early believers not only professed to be family. They *lived* as family!

In short, the church that is introduced in Scripture is a loving household, not a business. It is a living organism, not an organization. It is the corporate expression of Jesus Christ, not a religious corporation. It is the community of the King, not a well oiled, hierarchical machine.

These truths are not only set forth in the book of Acts. They are also peppered throughout all of Paul's epistles. And they reach their height in the letters of John.

In the language of the apostles, the church is composed of infants, little children, young men, brothers, sisters, mothers, and fathers—the speech and imagery of family (1 Cor. 4:15; 7:15; 1 Tim. 5:1-2; Jas. 2:15; 1 John 2:13-14).

The Simplicity of Christ

Tragically, Christianity has become something far removed from what it was in the first century. The church has become far too complex. It has fallen from its spiritual and heavenly position. It has regressed into something that better resembles a business rather than what God intended it to be—a close-knit community of Christ-like care and compassion. A community that is centered on Jesus Christ alone.

Paul's warning rings just as true today as it did in the first century:

For I am jealous over you with godly jealousy: for I have espoused you to one husband, that I may present you as a CHASTE VIRGIN to Christ. But I fear, lest by any means, as the serpent beguiled Eve through his subtlety, so your minds should be corrupted from THE SIMPLICITY THAT IS IN CHRIST. (2 Cor. 11:2-3)

Oh, the *simplicity* that is in Christ!

A.W. Tozer rightly put his finger on modern Christendom's obsession with power and trend toward complexity. Both of which undermine the Biblical vision of the church as family. He writes,

Churches run toward complexity as ducks take to water. What is back of this? First, I think it arises from a natural but carnal desire on the part of a gifted minority to bring the less gifted majority to heel and get them where they will not stand in the way of their soaring ambitions. The oft-quoted (and usually misquoted) saying is true of religion as well as in politics: 'Power tends to corrupt and absolute power tends to corrupt absolutely.' The itch to have the preeminence is one disease for which no natural cure has ever been found . . . In all our fallen life there is a strong gravitational pull toward complexity and away from things simple and real. There seems to be a kind of sad inevitability back of our morbid urge toward spiritual suicide. Only by prophetic insight, watchful prayer and hard work can we reverse the trend and recover the departed glory. (God Tells the Man Who Cares)

Our Lord longs for His people to return to the simplicity and purity that marked the early church. A simplicity and purity that are the chief characteristics of a vibrant, loving family.

Is this not the very longing that constantly yearns deep within the heart of every person? The desire to be a functioning part of a nurturing family? Is this not what our young people are aimlessly replacing with gangs, nightclubs, cults, unruly fraternities, wanton sororities, superficial sexual relationships and the like?

Put plainly, a church can have the most exhilarating praise music, the greatest orators, and the best evangelistic programs. But if it is not functioning as a close-knit family, then it cannot rightly be called a church! For love is the hallmark of the *ekklesia* (John 13:35).

Make no mistake about it. If we belong to Jesus Christ, then we belong to one another. Let us, therefore, *live* as the household of God. This cannot be done by human effort or zeal. It rather comes about naturally and organically as we begin to experience Christ corporately.

When we embrace Him in reality, we begin to embrace one another. And this is how the words of our Savior find their fulfillment: *"By this shall they know you are my disciples, if you have love one for another."*

CHAPTER 5

THE LEADERSHIP OF THE CHURCH: OVERSIGHT

The subject of leadership is one of the most pressing issues to address in any discussion of church practice. Every church has leadership. Whether a church has explicit or implicit leadership structures, leadership is always present.

In the words of Hal Miller, "Leadership *is*. It may be good or bad. It may be recognized and assented to or not. But it always is" (*"Nuts and Bolts of Leadership and Authority," Voices Newsletter, No.4*). Depending on who is doing the leading, leadership can be the church's worst nightmare or its greatest asset.

Because leadership has the potential of either becoming a cruel taskmaster or a useful servant, there is a tremendous need for Christians to take a fresh look at the subject. Let us begin our discussion by pointing out two different kinds of leadership. There is leadership that provides *oversight*. There is also leadership that provides *direction*. In this chapter, we will deal with oversight leadership. In the next, we will handle direction leadership.

Consider the following passages:

And from Miletus he sent to Ephesus, and called the ELDERS of the church . . . Take heed therefore unto yourselves, and to all the flock, over the which the Holy Ghost hath made you OVERSEERS to FEED THE CHURCH OF GOD, which he hath purchased with his own Blood. For I know this, that after my departing shall grievous wolves enter in among you, not sparing the flock. (Acts 20:17,28-29)

The ELDERS which are among you I exhort, who am also an elder, and a witness of the sufferings of Christ, and also a partaker of the glory that shall be revealed: FEED THE FLOCK OF GOD which is among you, taking THE OVER-SIGHT thereof, not by constraint, but willingly; not for filthy lucre, but of a ready mind; neither as being lords over God's heritage, but being ensamples to the flock. And when THE CHIEF SHEPHERD shall appear, ye shall receive a crown of glory that fadeth not away. (1 Pet. 5:1-4)

For this cause I left thee in Crete, that thou shouldest set in order the things that are wanting, and ordain ELDERS in every city, as I had appointed thee: If any is blameless, the husband of one wife, having faithful children not accused of dissipation or rebellion. For an OVERSEER must be blameless, as the steward of God; not selfwilled, not soon angry, not given to wine, not violent, not greedy for money. (Titus 1:5-7)

Elders, Shepherds, and Overseers

The above texts plainly show that the *oversight* of the church was placed in the hands of a group of people called "elders." The Greek word translated "elder" (*presbuteros)* simply means a mature man.

Elders, therefore, were local men who were more spiritually advanced than the rest. An elder ought never to be thought of as an office that is held vacant until filled. On the contrary, the elders were simply brothers—older men.

They were also called "overseers." This is a term that describes their function of supervising the affairs of the church. They were also called "shepherds" (or in some translations, "pastors"). This shows that they were responsible for instructing and guarding the flock from spiritual predators.

While all elders were "apt to teach" and had the gift of shepherding, not all who shepherded and taught were elders

(Titus 2:3-4; 2 Tim. 2:2,24; Heb. 5:12). Teaching could come from any believer who had a word of instruction for the church (1 Cor. 14:24-26).

Elders, then, were overseers and shepherds. The term "elder" refers to their *character*. The term "overseer" refers to their *function*. And the term "shepherd" refers to their *gifting*. Their chief responsibility was to supervise the believing community in times of crises.

While a discussion on the role of women in leadership is beyond the scope of this book, the NT seems to distinguish between *ministry* and *oversight*. The women of the early church freely functioned in every Spirit-endowed *gift*. But we never find them *superintending* the church in times of crises. Such a heavy burden seems to have fallen on the shoulders of the bro-thers—the women being spared!

Again, the sisters *ministered* through prophecy, instruction, exhortation, testimony, singing, encouragement, etc. But they are never seen doing the messy work of *overseeing* the church's problems (compare Acts 2:16-18; 18:26; 21:8-9; 1 Cor. 11:4-5; Gal. 3:28; Titus 2:3-4 with 1 Cor. 11:1-3; 14:34-35; 1 Tim. 2:11-15).

The Principle of Shared Oversight

The NT presents a vision of oversight that is shared. The apostles always established *plural* oversight within the churches they planted. It took at least fourteen years after the birth of the Jerusalem church for *elders* (plural) to emerge within it (Acts 11:30). A good while after they planted the four churches in South Galatia, Paul and Barnabas acknowledged *elders* (plural) in each of them (Acts 14:23).

Five years after Paul planted the church in Ephesus, he sent for the *elders* (plural) of the church to meet him in Miletus (Acts 20:17). When Paul wrote to the church in Philippi, now twelve years old, he greeted the *overseers* (plural) who were present

(Phil. 1:1). Finally, James summoned the sick to call for the *elders* (plural) of each of the churches in Judea (Jas. 5:14).

In addition, I offer this series of passages for consideration: Acts 11:29-30; 15:2-6,22-40; 20:17; 21:17-18; Eph. 4:11; 1 Thess. 5:12-13; 1 Tim. 4:14; 5:17-19; Titus 1:5; Heb. 13:7,17,24; 1 Pet. 5:1-2. Therein you will find that the Bible unshakeably demonstrates that a plurality of elders oversaw the early churches. No church in Century One had a single leader. There was no such thing as a modern pastor, priest, or bishop!

Those who point to the single leaders of the Old Testament to justify the popular practice of "sola pastora" (single pastor) make two mistakes. First, they overlook the fact that all of the single leaders of the Old Testament—Joseph, Moses, Joshua, David, and Solomon, etc.—were types of the Lord Jesus Christ, not a human officer.

Second, they ignore the pattern for oversight that is clearly spelled out throughout the entire NT. Watchman Nee observes,

The first question usually asked in connection with a church is, 'Who is the minister?' The thought in the questioner's mind is, 'Who is the man responsible for ministering and administering spiritual things in the church?' The clerical system of church management is exceedingly popular, but the whole thought is foreign to Scripture, where we find the responsibility for the church committed to elders, not to 'ministers,' as such; and the elders only take oversight of the church work, they do not perform it on behalf of the brethren. If, in a company of believers, the minister is active and the church-members are all passive, then that company is a mission, not a church. In a church all the members are active . . . He appointed some to take oversight of the work so that it might be carried on efficiently. It was never His thought that the majority of the believers should devote themselves exclusively to secular affairs and leave the church matters to a group of spiritual specialists. (The Normal Christian Church Life)

The elders in the NT all stood on an equal footing. Undoubtedly, some were more spiritually mature than the others. But there was no hierarchical structure among them. A careful reading of the book of Acts will show that while God often used different overseers as temporary spokesmen for specific occasions, no overseer occupied a permanent office of supremacy above the others.

Put differently, the modern offices of "senior pastor," "chief elder," and "head pastor" simply did not exist in the early church. The first-century believers did not mark off one man among the college of elders and elevate him to a superior position of authority.

The popular single pastor system of our day was utterly foreign to the NT church. Nowhere in the NT do we find one of the elders transformed into the status of a super-apostle and accorded with supreme administrative authority.

This degree of authority was only reserved for one person—the Lord Jesus Christ! He alone is the exclusive Head of the church. Only He has the supreme position of Commander and Chief. Not in rhetoric, but in reality!

Plural oversight in the church protected the sole Headship of Christ. It also served as a check against despotism and corruption among the overseers. As Watchman Nee says,

> *To have pastors in a church is Scriptural, but the present-day pastoral system is quite unscriptural; it is an invention of man . . . It is not God's will that one believer be singled out from all the others to occupy a place of special prominence, whilst the others passively submit to his will . . . To place the responsibility in the hands of several brethren, rather than in the hands of one individual, is God's way of safeguarding His church against the evils that result from the domination of a strong personality. (The Normal Christian Church Life)*

Function or Position?

So the oversight of the church was shared. But it was also *indigenous*. This means that the elders were local brothers who had been spiritually reared from within the church. Thus the accepted practice of importing a leader (typically a pastor) from another locality to lead a church has no basis in the NT. Instead, the elders were resident men whom God raised up from *within* the existing assembly.

Note that elders always emerged *long after* a church was born. There is no case anywhere in the NT where elders appear in an infant church. (Remember, an elder is a *seasoned* Christian.) And as with all gifts, the church produces elders. But it takes time for them to emerge. Consequently, house churches that get elders early on have no Scriptural backing.

Further, the workers in the first century acknowledged the elders after they had emerged. The elders did not install themselves. Sadly, this is rarely observed today.

Before elders emerged, the oversight of the church was in the hands of the apostolic worker who planted it (1 Thess. 2:7-12). Afterwards, it shifted to the hands of the elders.

An elder's authority to oversee was tied to his function and spiritual maturity. It was not tied to a sacerdotal office that was conferred upon him externally through an ordination service. After the Holy Spirit *chose* the elders, the apostolic workers later *confirmed* their calling publicly. But the function preceded the form (Acts 14:23; 20:28; Titus 1:5).

It is a tragic mistake, therefore, to equate the public acknowledgement of the workers with the establishment of a separate class system like the clerical profession of our day. Acknowledgement by the apostolic workers was no more than the public recognition of those who were already "elder-ing" in the church (see Num. 11:16 for this principle). It was not "ministerial ordination" as we know it today. The Greek words translated "ordain" in Acts 14:23 and Titus 1:5 simply mean to "acknowledge" someone that others have already endorsed. This means that the church trusted the elders.

Unfortunately, the American penchant for "offices" and "positions" has caused many believers to bring these ideas to the Biblical text and view the elders as official. Such thinking confuses the oversight of the early church with modern social conventions. It also strips the leadership terminology found in Scripture of its native meaning.

In the Greek, elder means mature man. Shepherd means one who nurtures and protects a flock. And overseer means one who supervises. Put plainly, the NT notion of oversight is *functional*, never *official*. Scripture never envisions overseers as "officers." In fact, it never speaks of church "offices" at all.

(In Acts 1:20; Rom. 11:13; 12:4; and 1 Tim. 3:1,10,13 the word "office" which appears in some translations has no equivalent in the Greek text. Further, Paul describes the overseer as a function. In the original, 1 Tim. 3:1 says "he that aspires to oversight desires a good *work*".)

True spiritual authority is based on *function*, not on *status*. It is rooted in spiritual life, not in title or position. In other words, NT leadership can best be understood in terms of *verbs* rather than *nouns*. Recall that our Lord Jesus rejected the authoritative pecking-orders of His day (Matt. 20:25-28; Luke 22:25-27). For in His eyes, spiritual authority is found in a towel and a basin, not in an external post (Matt. 23:8-12)!

Moral Characteristics

The elders mentioned in the NT were men of proven moral character, not extraordinary gifting (1 Tim. 3:1-7; Titus 1:5-9). They were servant-leaders (or as Robert Banks likes to say "leading-servants"), not slave-drivers (Matt. 20:25-26). They were men of proven spirituality and faithfulness, not high-powered administrators.

They were examples to the flock, not lords over it (1 Pet. 5:3). They functioned as bond-slaves, not as spiritual Caesars

(Luke 22:24-27). They were facilitators, not tyrants. They oversaw as fathers, not as despots (1 Tim. 3:4; 5:1).

They were persuaders of the truth, not ecclesiastical autocrats whose egos thrived on power (Titus 1:9). They were nurturers, not brow-beaters. Spiritual superintendents, not professional pulpiteers (Acts 20:28-35). They did not work instead of others, but supervised others as they worked.

NT elders were kingdom seekers, not empire builders. They were ordinary Christians, not multi-talented, ultra-versatile, superhuman, iconized, celebrity-like performers. Their qualification came not from professional schools or licenses. It came from the Spirit of God Himself (Acts 20:28).

Their training was not academic, formal, or theological; but practical and functional. For it was cultivated within the context of church life itself. The elders did not deem themselves qualified to oversee by acquiring a blend of accounting, public speaking, and amateur psychology skills. Their oversight was an organic, natural outgrowth of their life in the church and by real dealings of the cross.

First-century elders were not regarded as religious specialists, but as faithful and *trusted* brethren. They were not career clergy, but self-supporting family men with secular jobs (Acts 20:17,32-35; 1 Tim. 3:5; Titus 1:6; 1 Pet. 5:2-3).

Because of their tireless labor, some elders received double honor from the church. Just as the working ox deserves food and the working employee deserves payment, the elders who served well received double honor (1 Tim. 5:17-18).

Some have tried to argue for a professional clergy from this one isolated text. But the context of the passage reveals otherwise. First, the specific Greek words that the NT uses for "pay" or "wages" (*misthos* and *opsonion*) are not used here. The Greek word for "honor" in this passage is *time,* and it means to "respect" or "value" someone or something.

The same word is used four times in 1 Timothy. In every case, it means respect. God is to receive honor from man (1:17;

6:16), elders are to receive honor from the church (5:17), and masters are to receive honor from slaves (6:1). Another form of the word is used when Paul says that widows are to be honored by the church (1 Tim. 5:3). (Incidentally, *time* is never used in first-century literature to refer to "honorarium.")

Second, all believers are called to honor (*time*) one another (Rom. 12:10). It would be absurd to take this to mean that all believers are to receive payment from each other. Those elders who serve well are to receive more honor—or greater respect.

Third, the fact that respect is what Paul had in mind is born out by verse 19. Paul goes on to say that the elders are not to be accused (dishonored) unless there are two or three witnesses to confirm the accusation (1 Tim. 5:19).

Double honor may have included free-will offerings as a token of blessing from time to time (Gal. 6:6; 1 Tim. 5:17-18). But this was not the dominating thought. It is *honor* (respect) the elders deserve, not a salary! Consequently, 1 Timothy 5 is perfectly consistent with Acts 20:32-35. Both texts refer to the same people—the elders in Ephesus. (See also 2 Thess. 3:7-9 for the same principle.)

So the elders of the early church were not dependent on the church. Instead, they always made sure that they were in a position to give to it. They certainly did not receive a fixed salary like that of today's professional pastors. Nor were they Biblically sanctioned to receive full financial support like itinerant workers who traveled from region to region to plant churches (1 Cor. 9:1-18).

Because Paul was an itinerant worker, he had a legitimate right to receive full financial support from the Lord's people. But he intentionally waived this right whenever he worked with a group of Christians (1 Cor. 9:14-18; 2 Cor. 11:7-9; 12:13-18; 1 Thess. 2:6-9; 2 Thess. 3:8-9).

Paul waived this right because he did not want to financially burden any church while he served them. The Pauline principle regarding financial support can be summed up in the phrase:

"When I was *present* with you, I was chargeable to no one" (2 Cor. 11:9).

This principle uncovers the sober reality that the NT church knew nothing of a resident, hired clergy. Steve Atkerson skillfully isolates the point saying,

> *In Acts 20, Paul gave the Ephesian elders specific instructions on their duty as elders. Concerning finances, Paul stated that he had coveted no man's silver or gold and that he had paid his own way by 'working hard' with his hands (20:34-35; 18:1ff.). Following Paul's example, the elders were also to earn their living from a secular job so as to be able to help the weak and live out the words of the Lord Jesus that it is more blessed to give than to receive. Thus, from Acts 20:32-35 it is clear that elders are to be in the financial position of giving to the church, not receiving from it . . . Should the church employ professional pastors? Such an occupation was not only foreign to the NT church but was even discouraged (Acts 20:32-35) . . . creating a class of salaried ministers tends to elevate them above the average believer and fosters an artificial laity/clergy distinction. Finally, salesmen tend to be extra nice toward those to whom they hope to sell something. Hiring a career clergyman puts him in a similar salesman-customer relationship, and this, no doubt to some degree, affects his dealings with significant contributors. (Toward a House Church Theology)*

First-century elders did not take from God's people! They served them. Because they were simply brothers, the elders did not stand *over* the flock. Nor did they stand *apart* from it. Instead, they functioned as those who were *among* the flock (1 Pet. 5:1-3).

Note that the Greek word *proistemi* translated "over you" in 1 Thessalonians 5:12 carries the thought of one who stands *before* others rather than one who rules *over* them. The same is true for the texts in Hebrews 13:7,17,24. George Mallone insightfully remarks,

> *Contrary to what we would like to believe, elders, pastors, and deacons are not in a chain of command, a hierarchical pyramid, which puts them under Christ and over the church. The leaders of a Biblical church are simply members of the Body of Christ, not an elite oligarchy. They are members whom God has chosen to endow with certain charisms. (Furnace of Renewal)*

In keeping with our Lord's command, first-century elders did not permit themselves to be addressed by honorific titles like "Pastor Bill," "Elder Tom," "Bishop Jake," "Minister John," or "Reverend Sam" (Matt. 23:7-12). Such titles naturally elevate men to a plane above the other brethren in the church. For this reason, honorific titles are incompatible with NT Christianity.

Congregations and clergy alike are responsible for creating the current "Christian guruism" that is rampant in the Body today. Religious leaders are recast as spiritual celebrities and lauded with fan club status. Men are enthroned into offices that have no Biblical basis.

In stark contrast to this perversion, first-century elders were regarded as ordinary brethren. For that is exactly what they were—*brethren*! As such, they were just as approachable and accessible to the saints as was any other believer in the church. The common images of church overseers as "men of God" and sacred "men of the cloth" are utterly foreign to the Biblical concept!

The Modern Clergy System

It is an unmistakable tragedy that the dominating understanding of Christian leadership is couched in an institutional framework. Prevailing notions of clericalism have shaped our views regarding church leadership. The notion of an "ordained clergy" reflects hierarchical values. Such values are opposed to the spirit of the early church.

To be candid, the modern clergy/laity dichotomy is a post-Biblical concept that is devoid of any Scriptural warrant! It is also a bothersome menace to what God has called the church to be—a functioning Body! As Robert C. Girard says,

> *There is thoroughly entrenched in our church life an unbiblical two-caste system. In this two-caste system there is a clergy-caste which is trained, called, paid, and expected to do the ministering. And there is the laity-caste which normally functions as the audience which appreciatively pays for the performance of the clergy—or bitterly criticizes the gaping holes in that performance (and there are always gaping holes). No one expects much of the lower or laity caste (except attendance, tithe, and testimony). And everyone expects too much of the upper or clergy caste (including the clergy themselves!). The greatest problem in the whole business is the fact that the Bible's view of ministry totally contradicts this system. (Brethren, Hang Together)*

Writing in the same strain, Howard Snyder remarks,

> *The NT doctrine of ministry rests therefore not on the clergy-laity distinction but on the twin and complimentary pillars of the priesthood of all believers and the gifts of the Spirit. Today, four centuries after the Reformation, the full implications of this Protestant affirmation have yet to be worked out. The clergy-laity dichotomy is a direct carry-over from pre-Reformation Roman Catholicism and a throwback to the Old Testament priesthood. It is one of the principal obstacles to the church effectively being God's agent of the kingdom today because it creates a false idea that only 'holy men,' namely, ordained ministers, are really qualified and*

responsible for leadership and significant ministry. In the NT there are functional distinctions between various kinds of ministries but no hierarchical division between clergy and laity. (The Community of the King, used by permission of the author)

I will state it emphatically: NT elders were not clerical leaders! They were merely spiritually seasoned brethren given by the Holy Spirit to provide oversight (Acts 20:28-31; Titus 1:7-14; Heb. 13:17). And it took time for them to emerge.

While elders provided oversight, they did not monopolize the ministry of the church gatherings. Nor did they make decisions on behalf of the church (more on this later). Instead, they superintended the church as it experienced the rigors of life and the cross.

Please note that superintending is largely a passive role. The supervision of the elders did not stifle the life of the church. Nor did it interfere with the ministry of the other believers. While the gifted elders had a large share in teaching, prophesying and exhorting, they did so on the same footing as all the other members. They were not monopolizers.

In all these ways, the elders fleshed out the oversight of the early church without usurping the crown rights of Jesus Christ. And they did so without imposing a stranglehold upon the Lord's people!

In contrast to today's notion of "the pastor," NT elders did not operate like spiritual CEOs who presided over their spiritual enterprises—executing strategic programs in order to extend "their" congregations. Instead, the elders were fully aware that the church did not belong to them. It rather belonged to their beloved Master. He alone had the right to "walk in the midst of the lampstands." A first-century elder, therefore, would no doubt cringe if you used phrases like "his church" or "his people."

What I have said in the foregoing pages is not meant to cast a dim light on all clergy. Countless clergy have entered their profession with the highest motives. And I recognize that some of them have managed to keep themselves from the fleshly trappings that are attached to their profession.

The trouble lies not with clergy as people. It rather lies with the system to which they belong. The clergy profession is a mammoth institution that is far removed from the NT concept of leadership. And its mere presence hinders the cultivation of mature, relational, functioning churches that deeply express the Headship of Jesus Christ. As Jon Zens states,

> *While the 'clergy/laity' distinction is embedded and assumed in religious circles, it cannot be found in the NT . . . Because the NT knows nothing of 'clergy' the fact that a separate caste of the 'ordained' permeates our vocabulary and practice illustrates rather forcefully that we do not yet take the NT very seriously. The 'clergy' practice is a heresy that must be renounced. It strikes at the heart of the priesthood of all believers that Jesus purchased on the cross. It contradicts the shape that Jesus' kingdom was to take when He said, 'You are all brethren.' Since it is a tradition of man, it nullifies the Word of God . . . The clergy system stands as a monumental obstacle to genuine reformation and renewal. ("The 'Clergy/Laity' Distinction: A Help or a Hindrance to the Body of Christ," Searching Together, Vol. 23:4)*

Church Oversight and the Headship of Christ

Gathering up the content of what has been said, the overseers of the early church were simply *brethren*. Local family men. Mature and trustworthy servants of Christ. Proven men. Normal and ordinary Christians who cared for the flock.

With this in view, it is my hope that the Lord would shatter the unbiblical notion of the professional clergy system. This system has turned the precious things of the Lord into rank-and-file hierarchies, program-driven systems, and self-oriented institutions. Again, the Bible knows nothing of a separate class of ordained leaders (clergy) who rule over a lower class of believers (laity). Jon Zens argues,

> *The Roman Catholic 'clergy/laity' distinction was carried over in a different form in Protestantism. This unscriptural distinction has done, and is doing, untold harm . . . if we are sensitive to Scripture, we must abolish forever from our vocabulary the common distinction of 'clergy' ('the pastor') and 'laity' (the rest of the church). That distinction perpetuates an awful falsehood—but it does, unfortunately, reflect our thinking and practice by and large. ("What is a Minister?—Principles for the Recovery of N.T. Church Ministry," Searching Together, Vol. 11:3)*

The modern pastor system of Protestantism is a religious artifact that has allowed the Body of Christ to lapse into an audience due to its heavy reliance on a single leader. This unscriptural, clergy-dominated structure has done untold damage to God's people. It has turned church into the place where Christians watch professionals perform. It has transformed the holy assembly into a center for professional pulpiteerism supported by "lay-spectators."

The pastoral system has turned ministry into an elitist right. It has stolen your right to function as a member of the *ekklesia*! And it has lamed the believing priesthood! In short, the clergy concept of church leadership invariably crushes Body life. Christian Smith makes the point beautifully:

> *The clergy profession is fundamentally self-defeating. Its stated purpose is to nurture spiritual maturity in the church—a valuable goal. In actuality, however, it accomplishes the opposite by nurturing a permanent dependence of the laity on the clergy. Clergy become to their congregations like parents whose children never grow up,*

like therapists whose clients never become healed, like teachers whose students never graduate. The existence of a full-time, professional minister makes it too easy for church members not to take responsibility for the on-going life of the church. And why should they? That's the job of the pastor (so the thinking goes). But the result is that the laity remain in a state of passive dependence. Imagine, however, a church whose pastor resigned and that could not find a replacement. Ideally, eventually, the members of that church would have to get off of their pews, come together, and figure out who would teach, who would counsel, who would settle disputes, who would visit the sick, who would lead worship, and so on. With a bit of insight, they would realize that the Bible calls the Body as a whole to do these things together, prompting each to consider what gift they have to contribute, what role they could play to build up the Body . . . when we go back to the Word of God and read it afresh, we see that the clergy profession is the result of our human culture and history and not of God's will for the church. It is simply impossible to construct a defensible Biblical justification for the institution of clergy as we know it. ("Church Without Clergy," Voices in the Wilderness, Nov/Dec '88)

In the final analysis, the leadership of the church really comes down to one basic issue—the Headship of Christ. It rests upon the thorny question of who will be Head: Jesus Christ or men?

The pressing issue can be summed up thusly: Will we continue to affirm a system (clergy/laity) and an office (single pastor) that is absent from the NT? Or will we humbly set aside our human ideas of leadership in favor of Biblical principle?

What I have said in this chapter will no doubt raise eyebrows among those who read their Bibles with the shaded spectacles of modern clericalism. But let me be clear: The limitation that the modern clergy system imposes upon God's people is a solemn matter that constitutes no small scandal in the kingdom of God!

I have written these words in charity, not with a critical spirit. Therefore, I welcome neither a rash reaction nor a careless approval to what I have said. Instead, I challenge my readers to be drawn into a careful consideration of this subject. And to do their own prayerful thinking upon it.

Let us begin to recover and guard the Lord's unique place of sovereign Head in His church so that He may release His beloved priesthood (of *all* believers) from the chains that have bound it!

CHAPTER 6

THE LEADERSHIP OF THE CHURCH:
DIRECTION

In the last chapter we discovered that the accepted form of leadership in the Protestant church is utterly foreign to the NT. The commonly accepted "pastor" role is completely outside Biblical bounds. There is no such person mentioned in the NT.

According to the Biblical record, the oversight of the early church was placed into the hands of a group of local men who cared for the assembly. It was to them that God secured the task of guarding the flock. The Bible calls these men elders, overseers, and shepherds.

We also learned that the NT promotes no other form of leadership than a shared form. Yet the mere presence of a plurality of elders does not insure that a church will be healthy. If the elders do not oversee in the way that Christ prescribed, their effect can be more damaging than that of a single leader. Thus instead of a church having one spiritual tyrant, it will have several!

It is for this reason that the question of direction and decision-making in the church becomes crucial. Unlike the modern clergy system, first-century elders were never regarded as the prominent figures of the church.

In fact, there is a deafening lack of attention given to them throughout the NT. Paul's letters to the churches are never addressed to the elders. They are instead addressed to the *churches* themselves. (Note that in Philippians 1:1 Paul mentions the overseers only fleetingly—and only after he greets the church.) Further, Paul never even *mentions* elders in any of his epistles to the churches!

This omission is significant. For it vigorously challenges the Protestant notion of the preeminence of the pastor. It equally challenges the prevalent "house church" notion of the pre-eminence of the elders. Both ideas are at odds with Biblical teaching.

All of this shows that the subject of leadership gets far less air-play in the NT than it does in most Christian circles today. Think about the amount of ink—let alone blood—that has been spilt on the subject of leadership down through the centuries. Then compare it with how little air-time it gets in the NT. Such a discovery is rather shocking. It also demonstrates how far afield our priorities have been.

Yet the discovery also leads us to another inescapable point. That is, the main thrust of Paul's letters are centered on how the *whole church* is to bear responsibility for the flock.

Hierarchical, Positional, and Spiritual Authority

The Bible puts great stress on the fact that leadership in the kingdom of God is drastically different from leadership in both the Gentile and Jewish worlds. Unlike the Gentile notion of authority, the Christian approach to leadership does not link authority with rank-and-file power and hierarchical structures. NT leaders did not lord it over the saints through a fixed, chain-of-command hierarchy as did the leaders in the Gentile world (Matt. 20:25-28).

Unlike the Jewish notion of authority, the Christian approach to leadership does not link authority with outward ordination, office, position, title, or protocol. Leadership in the early church did not appeal to an authority vested in titular position as did leadership in the Jewish world (Matt. 23:1-12).

So the Christian orientation of leadership is unique to both the Gentile and Jewish mindsets. The Christian orientation links spiritual authority with spiritual function and maturity. It is based on the servant-leadership model that was a common theme in our Savior's teaching. A model that militates against the poisons of forced submission, top-heavy authority structures, and hierarchical relationships (Matt. 23:11; Mark 10:42-45; Luke 22:26-27).

In this context, the Christian model of leadership served as a safeguard to the real and living Headship of Christ. It was also a check against authoritarianism, formalism, and clericalism. The budding of Aaron's rod beautifully illustrates that the basis of spiritual authority rests upon resurrection life through spiritual service (Num. 17:1-11). It is never based on an assumed position.

The overseers of the early church, therefore, oversaw by example, not by coercion or manipulation. The respect they received from the congregation was in direct proportion to their sacrificial service (1 Cor. 16:10-11,15-18; Phil. 2:29-30; 1 Thess. 5:12-13; 1 Tim. 5:17). Their authority was rooted in their inward spiritual condition and outward function rather than in a sacerdotal position. In the words of Peter, they did not oversee by "being lords over God's heritage, but by being *examples* to the flock" (1 Pet. 5:3).

An example is a person who sets forth by his life a pattern for others to follow. Because elders were examples, they: 1) were active in ministry (for they set the example) and 2) encouraged the church to be just as active (for others followed their example).

Therefore, if an elder desired others to win the lost, it was incumbent upon him to model soul-winning. Why? Because he was an example! Consequently, the notion that holds that pastors do not win souls because "shepherds do not breed sheep, but sheep breed sheep" is a classic example of violently rupturing the Scripture!

If we push the shepherd-sheep metaphor beyond its intended meaning, we readily see its foolishness. Shepherds are incapable of breeding sheep. They also steal their wool and eat them for dinner! Unfortunately, not a few modern "shepherds" are guilty of feeding *upon* the sheep rather than feeding them (Jude 12, NIV; Ezek. 34:1-10).

Keep in mind that the early church meeting permitted each member to function in his or her gifts. It certainly did not promote passivity among the congregation while one man delivered a 45-minute sermon. Elders were not pulpiteers!

Simply put, oversight in the NT was not a slavish obligation nor a grim necessity. It was a valuable resource marked by humility, relatedness, servanthood, and godly example.

A Borrowed Leadership Paradigm

Today, the model that is often deployed for church leadership is drawn from the corporate business world. The paradigm used is a managerial one. Church leaders are taught to formulate a growth strategy and graphically chart out a plan to carry it out.

In other words, the modern church has gotten caught up in the stream-lined organizationalism of corporate American culture. The result? Christians have baptized secular leadership patterns and passed them off as being Biblically valid. Tragically, our modern notion of church leadership is culturally captive to the spirit of this age!

Seeing that the great weight of Biblical teaching on leadership has been lost to the prevailing notions of our culture, we must reclaim the Scriptural ground on the matter. It would do us well to remember that the chief metaphor that the Bible draws for the church is not *organization*, but *organism*. So the corporation metaphor is a distorted one.

As we have seen in Chapter 4, the chief metaphor for the church is the family. This explains why the Biblical image of leadership is that of a mother and a father (1 Thess. 2:6-12). Notwithstanding, even the parental image of leadership can become distorted and turned into cold prose if not viewed against the backdrop of the priesthood of *all* believers. Not to mention our primary relationship with one another as brothers and sisters (Matt. 23:8).

Plainly stated, leadership in the early church was non-hierarchical, non-aristocratic, non-authoritarian, non-institutional, and non-clerical. More importantly, God's idea of leadership is *functional, relational,* and *collective.*

To have the leadership of the church function according to the same principles as that of a corporate executive in a business or an aristocrat in an imperial caste-system was never our Lord's thought. It is for this reason that the NT authors never chose to use hierarchical and imperial metaphors to describe church leadership.

Images of slaves and children depict leadership rather than lords and masters (Luke 22:25-26). While this sort of thinking comes in direct conflict with today's popular idea of authority, it meshes perfectly with the Biblical teaching of the kingdom of God. The kingdom is the sphere in which the weak are strong, the poor are rich, the humble are exalted, and the last are first.

Rethinking Authority

The primary reason why our ideas on church leadership have strayed so far from God's thought can be traced to our tendency to project American political notions of government onto the Biblical writers—reading them back into the text. When we read words like "pastor," "overseer," and "elder," we immediately think in terms of governmental offices like "President," "Senator," and "Chairman."

So we regard elders, pastors, and overseers as sociological constructs (offices). We view them as vacancy slots that possess a reality independent of the persons that populate them. We then ascribe mere men with unquestioned authority simply because they "hold office."

The NT notion of leadership, however, is markedly different. There is no Biblical warrant for the idea that church leadership is official. Neither is there any Scriptural backing for the notion that some believers have authority over other believers! The only authority that exists in the church is Jesus Christ. Humans have no authority in themselves. Divine authority is only vested in the Head.

Authority in the NT is representative. This means that while believers can *represent* and *express* Divine authority, they never *assume* such authority. Insofar as a member of the Body is reflecting the mind of the Head, to that degree he is representing Divine authority.

Good leadership, therefore, is never authoritarian. It only displays authority when it is expressing the will of the Head. (For a fuller treatment on the NT concept of leadership, authority, and accountability, see my book *Who is Your Covering?*.)

The basic tasks of Biblical leadership are facilitation, nurture, and guidance. To the degree that a member is modeling the will of God in one of these areas, to that degree he or she is leading. Biblical leadership is service-oriented. Leaders excel in service and ministry. Therefore, they are examples to everyone else.

It is no wonder, therefore, that Paul never chose to use any of the forty plus common Greek words for "office" and "authority" when discussing elders. The startling reality is that Paul's favorite word for describing leadership is the opposite of what natural minds would suspect. It is *diakonos*, which means "a servant."

In his beautiful exposition of Mark 10:42-43, Ray Stedman remarks,

Authority among Christians is not derived from the same source as worldly authority, nor is it to be exercised in the same manner. The world's view of authority places men over one another, as in a military command structure, a business executive hierarchy, or a governmental system . . . Urged by the competitiveness created by the Fall, and faced with the rebelliousness and ruthlessness of sinful human nature, the world could not function without the use of command structures and executive decision. But as Jesus carefully stated, ' . . . it shall not be so among you.' Disciples are always in a different relationship to one another than worldlings are. Christians are brothers and sisters, children of one Father, and members one of another. Jesus put it clearly in Matthew 23:8, 'One is your Master, and all you are brethren.' Throughout twenty centuries the church has virtually ignored these words. Probably with the best of intentions, it has nevertheless repeatedly borrowed in total the authority structures of the world, changed the names of executives from kings, generals, captains, presidents, governors, secretaries, heads, and chiefs to popes, patriarchs, bishops, stewards, deacons, pastors, and elders, and gone merrily on its way, lording it over the brethren and thus destroying the model of servanthood which our Lord intended . . . Somewhere, surely, the words of Jesus, ' . . . it shall not be so among you,' must find some effect. Yet in most churches today an unthinking acceptance has been given to the idea that the pastor is the final voice of authority in both doctrine and practice, and that he is the executive officer of the church with respect to administration. But surely, if a pope over the whole church is bad, a pope in every church is no better! ("A Pastor's Authority," Discovery Paper #3500, Discovery Publishing)

Let us never forget that the elders were servants of the Master, the Lord Jesus. He alone owned the rights to the church. Consequently, the NT never refers to an elder (shepherd) or apostle as "the head" of a church! Such a title is exclusively reserved for the Lord Jesus. He alone is the Head of His Body. And the church has no heads under His own!

Since the elders of the early church knew the church did not belong to them, they did not have their own agendas to push. Nor did they roadblock others into mindless submission by an appeal to their "authority." The elders of the early church did not operate as an oligarchy (absolute rule by a few). Nor as a dictatorship (monarchical rule by one person). Again, they were simply older men whom the church organically and naturally looked to in times of crises.

By the same token, the early church did not operate like our contemporary democracy. Many mistakenly think that our American democratic system is rooted in Biblical theology. But there isn't a single example in the entire NT where church decisions were made by a show of hands.

The Divine Rule of Consensus

So what was the NT pattern for direction and decision-making in the church? It was simply by the consensus of the entire assembly. "Then it seemed good to the apostles and elders, *with the whole church*" and "it seemed good *to us*, having come to *one mind*" is the Divine model for managing church affairs (Acts 15:22,25). In other words, the direction and decision-making of the church was not in the hands of the elders. It was in the hands of *all* the brothers and sisters!

Because the church is a Body, all of its members must agree before it can move forward in obeying the Head (Rom. 12:4-5; 1 Cor. 12:12-27; Eph. 4:11-16). In fact, a lack of unity and cooperation among the members reveals a failure to embrace the Head.

Majority rule and dictatorial rule do violence to the Body image of the church. And it dilutes the unvarnished testimony that Jesus Christ is the Head of one unified Body. For this reason Paul's epistles to the churches are saturated with exhortations to be of one mind (Rom. 15:5-6; 1 Cor. 1:10; 2 Cor. 13:11; Eph. 4:3; Phil. 2:2; 4:2).

Recall how our Lord Jesus taught that if His people would agree on something, the decision would carry His Father's authority (Matt. 18:19). Significantly, the word "agree" in this text is translated from the Greek word *sumphoneo*.

Sumphoneo means to sound together—to be in one accord. Our word "symphony" is derived from this Greek term. So the meaning is clear. When the church is in sympathetic harmony with the Divine mind, God must act.

Consensus mirrors the inseparable union of the eternal Godhead, whose nature we are called to reflect. God acts when Father, Son, and Spirit agree. He also acts when the church agrees—and not a particular section of it.

Even in the Old Testament economy, the Bible associates consensus with spiritual fullness (1 Chron. 12:38-40; 13:1-4; 2 Chron. 30:4-5). Conversely, it associates divided judgment with spiritual ruin (1 Kings 16:21-22). In short, the Bible presents consensus as the Divine mode of decision-making in the church.

So when a church is fully established, the direction comes from the entire Body. Not from a man or a special group of men. Before the church is birthed, however, direction comes from the apostolic worker—the person who founded it. (See *Who is Your Covering?* for details.) But after the foundation is laid, direction shifts to the hands of the whole church. (*Oversight* shifts to the elders when they emerge.)

While the ministry of the apostolic worker ought always to be welcomed in the church, the spiritual responsibility for the assembly eventually turns to the whole church (Acts 14:23; 20:28-31; 1 Tim. 5:17; Titus 1:5; Heb. 13:17). Thus the concept of an extra-local, centralized headquarters does not exist in the NT. In the first century, each church was *spiritually unified* by life. But they were *self-governing* and *autonomous* by locale.

The first-century churches were independent in organization and responsibility. But they were interdependent in life and unity. This is God's wonderful design. For when an extra-local apostle takes control of a local assembly, it becomes nothing more than an extension of himself. As a result, the church turns into a sect. And the full testimony of Jesus that it is supposed to bear becomes obscured.

Again, the elders of the early church bore the bulk of spiritual oversight and pastoral care for the assembly (Heb. 13:7,17,24). But they did not make decisions on behalf of the church. Nor did they supply the church's direction. There is no evidence from Scripture to support such notions.

Therefore, an elder has no Biblical or spiritual right to bark out commands to a passive congregation. Instead, the elders (once they emerged) work together with the whole church toward reaching a *unanimous* decision and a *single* mind (Acts 15:22,28). It is the church, as a whole, that makes the decisions as one new man.

But what of Hebrews 13:17? There the author says "obey them that are over you." In the original, the meaning is to "allow oneself to be persuaded."

The Greek word for obey in this passage is not *hupakuo*, the garden-variety word for obedience used elsewhere. It is *peitho* [middle-passive form] which means to yield to persuasion. The author of Hebrews is simply saying "allow yourselves to be persuaded by those who are more mature in Christ than you are."

So within the decision-making process of the early church, the role of the elders was to help the church reach an undivided judgment on a matter. By virtue of their relative spiritual maturity, they were sometimes able to persuade the church into a unified understanding of the Lord's mind. But they had no right to force the church to adopt their view.

NT elders were men who demonstrated qualities which encouraged and built family solidarity (1 Tim. 3:4-5; Titus 1:6). But they had no special authority to make decisions or give direction. They, along with the entire church, bore the responsibility for direction and decision-making. No more, no less.

The Meaning of Consensus

Let us examine the meaning of consensus for a moment. A church reaches a consensus when all its members have come to a unanimous agreement in support of a particular decision. Consensus and unanimity are virtually identical.

Granted, the church may agree with a decision with varying degrees of enthusiasm (some consenting "with a heavy heart"). Yet a consensus is reached when all have unanimously come to the place where they have set aside their objections. And all can support the decision in good conscience.

When a church operates by consensus, decisions are delayed until full agreement is reached. Such a process requires that all the members equally participate in and accept responsibility for reaching the mind of the Lord on a given matter. (Incidentally, the mind of Christ does not belong to an individual. It is a corporate discovery.)

Consequently, when the church reaches a consensus, murmuring and complaining are eliminated. Why? Because every member has had an equal share in the decision. The church owns the decision. It was made by the church. It was made for the church. In the words of Christian Smith,

Consensus is built on the experience of Christian community. It requires strong relationships able to tolerate struggling through issues together. It requires mutual love and respect to hear each other when there is disagreement. Consensus also requires a commitment to know and understand other people more than a desire to convince or railroad them. Consensus, as a way to make decisions in the church, is not easier, just better. To paraphrase Winston Churchill, consensus is the worst form of decision-making in the church, except for all the others. Consensus is not strong on efficiency, if by that we mean ease and speed. It can take a long time to work through issues, which can become quite frustrating . . . consensus is strong on unity, communication, openness to the Spirit's leading, and responsible participation in the Body. In achieving those values, consensus is efficient. Deciding by consensus, then, simply requires belief that unity, love, communication, and participation are more important in the Christian scheme than quick, easy decisions. It requires the understanding that, ultimately, the process is as important as the outcome. How we treat each other as we make decisions together is as important as what we actually decide. (Going to the Root)

Pragmatism is the American philosophy that says "if it works, it is good; if it produces results, it is true." Those who look through the prism of pragmatism regard consensus to be idealistic and impractical. Yet it is the only sure safeguard to ensure that we have obtained the mind of Christ. Some may retort that this method would never work in our day. But the testimony of church history defies them.

Decision-making by consensus has been the practice of the Hutterites, the Quakers, and the Open Brethren (the Muller-Lang strand), and the Little Flock. Many modern house churches also practice it. To be sure, consensus is *humanly* impossible. But so is salvation (Matt. 19:26)!

The indwelling Spirit makes decision-making by consensus a practical reality and a fruitful testimony to the indivisible life of Christ. The testimony of one writer is most enlightening on this score:

As one who has been connected with this church [Bethesda church in Bristol] for the last sixty years, I very gladly testify that I firmly believe that simple obedience to the directions of the Word of God on this subject has been one of the chief causes of the remarkably uninterrupted peace and harmony which, through the goodness of God, have characterized this church all these years. The reason is not far to seek. The plan of waiting, before coming to a decision regarding any step, until the indwelling Holy Spirit has brought all minds into unity of purpose, yields to our Lord Jesus Christ His proper place as the One Lord and Master in His House, and keeps us His brethren in our proper place of humility, dependence, and subjection. (The Churches of God)

The Challenge Before Us

The disconnect between the modern church's practice of decision-making and the NT reality is indeed profound. It should give us pause to question why we have strayed so far. Could it be that the problem of church splits, wandering sheep, and unresolved power struggles is directly due to our arrogant conclusion that we have found a better way to lead God's house in the 20th century?

In many institutional churches, the pastor (and sometimes "the board") makes decisions independent of the church. The same is true in house churches where elders rule in clerical fashion. They decide without any regard for the concerns or judgments of the believers. Members are without a voice in the church's affairs. What is more, they are encouraged to "go elsewhere" if they do not "line up!"

In those churches that decide on the basis of majority rule, those who "lose the vote" are left to question the judgment of the populace. Sometimes they are left to question the very ethics of the procedure. The fact that Scripture is filled with examples where the majority was wrong is conveniently overlooked. Arguing on the basis of Matthew 18:18-20, Robert Banks observes,

> *Guidance on matters affecting the community's life was principally granted to members when they met together to discern what God required of them. They received this guidance from the Spirit through their exercise of gifts of knowledge, revelation, wisdom, and so on. In all this Paul never tires of insisting that every member of the community has the responsibility to impart the particular insights they have been given. All are encouraged to 'instruct one another,' to 'speak God's Word . . . so that all may learn and be encouraged,' and to 'teach and admonish one another in all wisdom,' for it is through 'speaking the truth*

in love' that they are to 'grow up in every way into Him who
is the Head, even Christ.' Thus, the most characteristic
setting in which the community received guidance was when
Christians assembled to share and evaluate the gifts given to
them. Here, in a variety of complimentary ways, guidance
was conveyed through each to all and through all to each.
(Paul's Idea of Community)

There is no doubt that consensus is costly. It imposes responsibility upon *all* the members to seek the Lord for themselves. It equally demands that each believer patiently wrestle
and struggle *with one another* to secure the Lord's mind.

Consensus often means trading quick decisions for gaining
confidence through delay. But, oh, what building together it
affords! What working out of patience! What expression of
mutual love and respect! What exercise of Christian community!
What restraint imposed upon the flesh! What bearing of the
cross! And what dying to our own agendas!

Is such a cost not worth the value of securing the Lord's
thought for His Body? Is it not worth giving Him opportunity to
work in us more deeply as a people? Does not confidence in
getting the mind of the Lord on a matter relating to *His* church
(not ours) outweigh the convenience of making hasty decisions?
Decisions that can damage the lives of our brethren and miss the
Lord's will. We so often forget that in God's eyes, the means is
just as important as the end.

In approaching the matter of consensus, some have sacrificed
God's truth upon the altar of convenience. They have cried out,
"Is consensus practical?" "Is it possible?" "Is it expedient?"

In God's thought such questions are both irrelevant and
(often) irreverent. Expediency is a dangerously thin criterion for
judging actions in the spiritual realm.

Therefore, the core question that must be asked is not "Is this
expedient," but "Is this Scriptural?" You can rest assured that if
the Lord has bid us to follow something, it will be both possible
and practical by His grace.

In summary, leadership in the early church did the following. It encouraged every member to exercise his or her gifts. It helped to form a spiritual solidarity among the believers. It fostered a sense of community, cohesion, and unity within the church.

The ability to wield power or impose one's will on others does not characterize Biblical leadership. Leadership is characterized by the ability to weld the church together to reach undivided judgments on critical affairs. Any person who does this at a given time is being a leader at that moment.

All in all, the NT knows nothing of an authoritative mode of leadership. Nor does it know a "leaderless" egalitarianism. It rejects both hierarchical structures as well as rugged individualism. Instead, the NT envisions leadership as coming from the *entire church*! Direction and decision-making are supplied by the brothers and sisters by consensus. Oversight is supplied by the seasoned brothers.

Biblical leadership is simply one of the many Spirit-endowed gifts enumerated in the NT (1 Cor. 12:28). And as is the case with all other gifts, leadership is always exercised in the context of mutual subjection rather than in a hierarchical structure of subordination (Eph. 5:21; 1 Tim. 5:19-20).

CHAPTER 7

THE ETERNAL PURPOSE

In this chapter we will consider the over-arching purpose of the church. For reasons that I will presently state, God did not form the church to be an end in itself. The church is a means for the fulfillment of something far greater.

God's Highest Intention

In Ephesians 3:11, Paul pens a phrase that is pregnant with meaning: *the eternal purpose*. Throughout his mighty Ephesian epistle, Paul spills a great deal of ink unveiling the eternal purpose of God to the believers in Asia Minor.

In fact, the entire letter is a breath-taking unfolding of the Divine purpose. In it, Paul puts the most sublime truths into human words. The ultimate intention that God has had in His heart from ages past is richly set forth in Ephesians.

And what is this exceedingly high and all-governing purpose? It is nothing short of the universal fullness of Jesus Christ. That is, God has purposed that His glorious Son fill all things in the universe and that all things be summed up in Him (Eph. 1:9-10; 4:10; Col. 1:15-20).

Remarkably, Paul tells us that God has chosen the church to be the vessel for the full expression and realization of this glorious purpose (Eph. 1:22-23; 2:19-22; 3:8-13; 4:8-16; 5:23-32). The central aim of the church, then, is to realize the eternal purpose of God.

Properly conceived, the church exists to make the fullness of Christ known on the earth. It stands here to register Christ's final victory over Satan in every place (Eph. 3:9-10). As His Body, the church is here to express Jesus in all of His glory. For what is the purpose of a body, but to express the life in it?

This means, among other things, that the church is called to carry on the earthly ministry of Jesus Christ. It exists for the fulfillment of God's aged-long quest to find a resting place for Himself. For the church embodies God's very presence.

In a word, the church is Jesus Christ in corporate human expression (1 Cor. 12:12)! Without the church, our Lord Jesus would have no way to express Himself on the earth. The church is the Body of Christ locally expressed and visibly functioning. It is here to fulfill God's original purpose to secure a corporate man to express His image and bear His rule (Gen. 1:26-28). It is here to make Jesus Christ, who is the image of God, visible again!

Close scrutiny of the Biblical text demonstrates that every principle stated in the NT regarding our corporate life rests upon this all-consuming vision. Each principle for church practice set forth in Scripture was established by God with a view to the building together of a people into the likeness of His Son. Consider the following passages:

> *. . . [You are] called according to HIS PURPOSE . . . TO BE CONFORMED TO THE LIKENESS OF HIS SON, that He might be the Firstborn among MANY BROTHERS. (Rom. 8:28-29, NIV)*

> *My dear children, for whom I am again in the pains of childbirth until CHRIST IS FORMED IN YOU. (Gal. 4:19, NIV)*

> *In Him THE WHOLE BUILDING IS JOINED TOGETHER AND RISES TO BECOME A HOLY TEMPLE IN THE LORD. And in Him YOU TOO ARE BEING BUILT TO-GETHER TO BECOME A DWELLING IN WHICH GOD LIVES BY HIS SPIRIT. (Eph. 2:21-22, NIV)*

> *. . . To prepare God's people for works of service, so that THE BODY OF CHRIST MAY BE BUILT UP until we all*

reach unity in the faith and in the knowledge of the Son of God and BECOME MATURE, ATTAINING TO THE WHOLE MEASURE OF THE FULLNESS OF CHRIST. (Eph. 4:12-13, NIV)

. . . As Christ loved the church and gave Himself up for her TO MAKE HER HOLY, CLEANSING HER by the washing with water through the word, and TO PRESENT HER TO HIMSELF AS A RADIANT CHURCH, WITHOUT STAIN OR WRINKLE OR ANY OTHER BLEMISH, BUT HOLY AND BLAMELESS. (Eph. 5:25-27, NIV)

For it became Him, for whom are all things, and by whom are all things, IN BRINGING MANY SONS TO GLORY . . . (Heb. 2:10)

The House of God

Mark it down. God is not after a pile of individual and isolated stones! He is seeking to obtain a people who are *built together* with His life. Through Christ's death, we have all been hewn out of the same Rock to become individual "living stones." But through His resurrection, the Spirit has come to cement us together to form one spiritual house!

Yet the mere gathering together of a heap of building materials into one place does not make a building. The building that God seeks for His dwelling is only formed when each living stone is properly fitted together and inseparably joined to other living stones. This is the church.

The intention of God lies in securing local bodies of believers that are growing corporately into the Head. Believers who are rubbing against one another and bearing the cross together. In short, the church is simply Jesus Christ reproducing Himself in the lives of men and women . . . collectively.

Regrettably, the American obsession with individualism and independence has shaped the minds of many modern Christians.

As a result, they have been blinded from seeing that God's ultimate intention rests upon the formation of a spiritual community.

Hal Miller has made the incisive point that the American venom of individualism has infiltrated the modern evangelical mindset—preventing it from grasping the higher purpose of God. He writes,

> *Americans see the isolated individual as the source of all moral virtue and society as nothing more than a collection of these individuals. Evangelicalism implicitly agreed. It spoke eloquently of saving individuals; but it did not take seriously what these individuals were saved into. They preached the gospel of the individuals rightly enough; but as true Americans, they did not see that God might intend to go further and make a people out of these persons. Evangelicalism sought to transform people and so transform the world. They did not see that something might be missing from this vision, something their assumption of American individualism would hide from them. The true Christian vision is to transform people, transforming them into a people, and so transform the world. The evangelicals missed that middle term. They could not see the church as a foretaste of the new society; it was a club for the new individuals. The evangelicals simply dressed American individualism in Christian clothing. They ended up with the new isolated individuals, but in the old society. ("The Uneasy Conscience of Modern Evangelicalism," Voices in the Wilderness, July '86)*

Individualism and independence are the enemies of Body life! This is not to say that we are to reject our *individuality*. We should welcome our unique gifting and temperament as individual members of the Body.

At the same time, we are to reject the fleshly tendency to see ourselves as entities that exist over and above the community (individualism). And we are to denounce the carnal urge to live and act without regard to our fellow-brethren (independence). In the words of Paul, "The eye cannot say to the hand I have no need of you, or again, the head to the foot, I have no need of you" (1 Cor. 12:21).

Most of the NT is written to Christian communities rather than to individuals. For this reason we lose a great deal when we read our Bibles with the lens of modern, self-oriented individualism. Many vital truths in Scripture can only be rightly grasped when we understand them within the context of a corporate community. For they can only be fulfilled by such a community—the very audience for whom the NT authors wrote.

In short, the Bible forcefully makes the point that the Christian life can only be successfully fleshed out when we are living in close interdependent fellowship with other believers. Consequently, when we understand that the NT text was set within the context of a community, it sheds tremendous light on the meaning of every passage. It also delivers us from the Protestant fallacy of individualizing Paul's corporate exhortations.

A Fitly Framed Temple

While the institutional church does a good job of protecting us from one another, the church of Jesus Christ is designed to rid us of *self*. It does so by bringing us into intimate contact with our fellow brethren.

Stated simply, the early church was profoundly relational. Believers were being knitted together continuously (Eph. 4:16; Col. 2:19). For this reason those who meet according to NT lines often encounter the cross in one another as they seek to dwell as one Body (Eph. 4:1-3).

Because we are fallen, we find ourselves suffering with one another. But such suffering is an instrument of His cross. And it is designed to transform us. As we meet the cross in one another, dying to ourselves, the Spirit of God begins the wonderful process of forming Christ into us corporately.

Recall how the acacia boards in the tabernacle of old had to be cut, shaped, and fitted together to make up the house of God. So it is with the church today. We all must undergo the cutting of the cross if we will be "builded together" to form God's habitation (Eph. 2:22).

The church, therefore, is not a collection of isolated Christian units meeting together as a congregation. Never! The church is a company of Christ-indwelt men and women who are being formed together by the power of the Holy Spirit. For this reason, the church cannot be measured by individual units alone. It is a *corporate* life. A *collective* spiritual organism.

One brick never made a temple yet, nor has a heap of bricks piled one on top of the other. The church is a people built together into one new man. And it exists to be the corporate expression of Christ.

We may also say that the church is the school of Christ. It is the laboratory of the redeemed where the necessary lessons of interdependence, interrelatedness, suffering, self-denial, forbearance, meekness, kindness, and love are learned. The church is the habitat where living the Christ-life is tested, fleshed out, and eventually mastered.

Corporate conformity to Christ is the central feature of the purpose of God. And the church is the Divinely-ordained environment (or habitat) for this transformation to occur. The purpose of the church, therefore, transcends the kindergarten notion of being a "soul-winning station." The idea that the church is a "soul-winning station" is an aberrant view of the *ekklesia*.

According to the NT, souls are saved so they can be added to the church. Modern evangelicalism has reversed this order. It has put the salvation of souls ahead of the building of the church. Interestingly, there is far more NT support for the building up of the Body than there is for the evangelization of sinners.

Again, God's goal is the increase of Christ. When souls are won and added to the church, Christ is enlarged (Acts 2:47; 5:14; 11:24). From God's perspective, this is the goal of winning souls. Even so, whenever we view the church in strictly individualistic terms, we lose sight of the greater purpose of God.

A Glorious Bride

From Genesis to Revelation, the Bible contains a central motif that runs throughout its pages like an unbroken cord. This motif was shrouded in a mystery and hid in God for ages. It was revealed in the Old Testament through types and shadows. And it was made known in the NT—especially in the letters of Ephesians and Colossians.

Paul was the first to unveil this mind-boggling mystery (Eph. 3:3-9; 6:19; Col. 1:26-29; 4:3). What is this mystery? That God has been preparing a Bride for His beloved Son.

In Genesis, Eve prefigures the Bride of Christ. God gave her to Adam to be his perfect counterpart (Gen. 2:18-25; Rom. 5:14; Eph. 5:31-32). We meet this Bride again at the end of Revelation. Only now she has developed into a glorious city (Rev. 21:2,9)!

Both the woman in Genesis and the woman in Revelation point to the glorious church that the Father is seeking to obtain for His Son (2 Cor. 11:2; Eph. 5:22-32). And this Bride will eventually become one with God (1 Cor. 15:28; Rev. 21-22). That is, the Bride of the Lamb will become the Wife of the Lamb!

Like Eve, the church is the counterpart of Jesus Christ. She was *in* Him from the beginning. She came *out* of Him in space-time. And she will go back *into* Him in the future. The church is inseparable from her Lord.

Like the city, the church bears His glorious image and exhibits His sovereign rule. The purpose of the church, therefore, is to make "herself ready" so that Christ, the Bridegroom, will return for her (John 3:29-30; Rev. 19:7). She does this by loving Him, just as any bride loves her bridegroom.

A Golden Lampstand

In the book of Revelation, the purpose of the church is brought into sharp focus from another plane. Therein we discover that in God's thought, each church is represented by a lampstand all of gold (Rev. 1:20). Let us briefly consider the chief features of the lampstand.

First, the lampstand has a distinct image. It is not a nebulous mass. It contains seven branches. Three on each side connected to a central stem. This speaks of plurality in oneness.

In addition, it has three flowers and three almond cups on each of its seven branches. The flowers emerging out of the almond cups represent life emerging out of death. The number three symbolizes resurrection. The lampstand points to the Risen Christ, who is the only Person in the Godhead that bears an image (2 Cor. 4:4; Col. 1:15; Heb. 1:3).

Second, the lampstand is the bearer of oil and light. Oil speaks of the Holy Spirit. And light is a shadow of the truth that He imparts. Third, the lampstand consists of gold, which is an apt symbol of God the Father—the Source of all things.

The lampstand, therefore, is a portrait of the Triune God, whose fullness dwells in Jesus Christ (Col. 2:9). From the book of Revelation we discover that the purpose of the lampstand is to shine its light upon the glorious Person of Christ (Rev. 1:13-16).

Herein lies the purpose of the church. The church exists to show forth Jesus Christ. To make Him known. Putting it in Scriptural terms, the church is called to bear "the testimony of Jesus" (Rev. 1:2,9; 6:9; 12:11,17; 19:10).

In order for the church to bear the Divine testimony, it must, like the creation of the lampstand, be molded into the image of Christ by the hammer of God's discipline. Through the anvil of the cross and the refining fires of suffering, the church becomes conformed to the image of Jesus. (Note that the lampstand of the Mosaic tabernacle was said to be made of "beaten" gold.)

Such is the cost of living in *real* church life. This is opposed to the artificial superficiality that is endemic to the institutional church. Yet the peaceable fruit of genuine Body life is the full expression of God's glory in a corporate earthen vessel (2 Cor. 4:4-12).

Everything that God does is controlled by His ultimate end. Paul tells us that God works *all things* according to the counsel of His purpose (Eph. 1:11). Every spiritual principle for church life is hinged upon this all-inclusive and all-governing intention.

The Divine aim for the church is that she embody the character of the Lord Jesus Christ corporately. And when she does, people encounter God whenever they touch the church (1 Cor. 14:24-25).

Recall that the temple of old was the meeting place between God and man. In like manner, when the church gathers under Christ, the Lord is there. He is made visible. He is revealed. Such is the purpose of the church.

A Kingdom Community

Another aspect of the church's purpose is summed up in our Lord's oft-repeated phrase, "the kingdom of God." The kingdom of God is the reign of God. And God reigns in the hearts of men and women whenever they enthrone His Son—*the* King (Matt. 25:34; Luke 1:33; Rev. 17:14; 19:16).

When Jesus was on earth, His ministry was chiefly centered on extending the reign of God. As He preached the gospel, healed the sick, cast out demons, raised the dead, fed the poor, reproved oppressors, and trained His disciples, He destroyed Satan's work on the one hand and extended His Father's reign on the other (Matt. 4:23; 12:28-29; Acts 10:38; 1 John 3:8).

As the community of the King, the church exists to carry on the earthly ministry of Jesus (Matt. 18:19-20; Mark 16:15-20). As the corporate expression of the Risen Christ, the church is called to advance God's reign and destroy Satan's work (Matt. 10:7-8; 16:17-20; 18:18-20; Luke 10:18-20; John 14:12).

As the recipient of the out-poured Spirit, the church is equipped to fulfill the mission of Christ. She "preaches the gospel to the poor, heals the brokenhearted, preaches deliverance to the captives, recovers sight to the blind, sets at liberty them that are bruised, and preaches the acceptable year of the Lord" (Luke 4:18-21). In short, the kingdom of God is embodied in the Person of Jesus. And the church is the instrument for its earthly expression.

To be sure, the kingdom of God will one day come upon this earth physically and visibly (Dan. 7:13-14; Isa. 9:6-7; Rev. 11:15; 1 Cor. 15:24-28; 2 Tim. 4:1). Yet today the kingdom is present spiritually and in a mystery (Matt. 13:1ff.; Mark 4:11; Luke 8:10; 17:20-21). Whenever Christ is exercising His authority and manifesting His presence, the kingdom of God is present. Even though it is still future (Luke 16:16; 17:20; Rom. 14:17; 1 Cor. 4:20).

So the kingdom of God is both heavenly and earthly. Both hidden and being revealed. Both future and present. To borrow a phrase from one NT scholar, the kingdom is "already" but "not yet" here (Heb. 6:5).

As the agent of the kingdom, the church moves upon the earth as a visible, countercultural community. It is a new social reality that exercises Christ's authority and bears His image—the two tasks that God called man to fulfill in the beginning (Gen. 1:26-28).

Because the goal of the kingdom is to sum up all things in Christ and establish God's reign, our Lord's radical teachings on "the kingdom" and Paul's majestic vision of the "eternal purpose" are fundamentally the same. As Howard Snyder observes,

The church is seen as the community of God's people—a people called to serve Him and called to live together in true Christian community as a witness to the character and values of His kingdom. The church is the agent of God's

mission on earth. But what is that mission? It is nothing other than bringing all things and, supremely, all people of the earth under the dominion and Headship of Jesus Christ . . . Jesus speaks of the kingdom of God; Paul speaks of God reconciling all things through Jesus Christ (2 Cor. 5:19; Col. 1:20). These are two ways of saying the same thing, for God is reigning and reconciling through Christ . . . Jesus speaks of 'the mystery of the kingdom'; Paul speaks of 'the mystery of Christ.' For Christ is the key to the kingdom. The kingdom of God is the ongoing reconciliation work of God in Christ seen from the perspective of the final definitive establishment of God's dominion when Christ returns to earth. Christ must return to fully establish His kingdom. But by His Spirit He now works on earth through His Body, the church . . . What then is the kingdom of God? It is Jesus Christ and, through the church, the uniting of all things in Him . . . The Scriptures emphasize the eternal purpose or plan or will of God, that which He is doing in history to bring about the reconciliation of all things. This Divine purpose is identified with the kingdom or reign of God. (The Community of the King, used by permission of the author)

Watchman Nee underlines the same point saying,

. . . Not only where the Lord Jesus is, but also where the church is, the kingdom of God is. Not only does the Lord Jesus Himself represent the kingdom of God, the church also represents the kingdom of God. The important point here is not a matter of future reward or position in the kingdom, whether large or small, high or low. The concern is not with these things. The vital matter is that God wants the church to represent the kingdom of God. The work of the church on earth is to bring in the kingdom of God. All the work of the church is governed by the principle of the kingdom of God. (The Glorious Church)

Tension Between Wine and Wineskin

Every practice of the early church has been established by God to display His eternal purpose. Hence, we have no right to change any of them. At the same time, it is not the mere employment of "NT patterns" that God is after today. But the higher purpose that undergirds every practice.

Therefore, let us not put undue stress upon the wineskin (church practice) to the neglect of the wine (Jesus Christ in the Spirit). To have a proper wineskin without the wine is to miss God's highest intention. Over-emphasis on the wineskin produces churches that are characterized by a dead orthodoxy and a dry-as-dust scholastic approach to the Bible.

In churches of this ilk, the texture of church life is stale and mechanical. It is hollow and wooden. The church's unhealthy obsession with external correctness and correct doctrine squelches the necessary features of vibrancy, freshness, richness, and life. The result is that the Spirit of God becomes the prisoner of an institutionalized system.

While the tendency of our flesh is to turn the precious things of God into legal methods and tightly-held formulas, God's way of working is always by the Spirit and by life. Let us not forget that the church is composed of "living" stones who offer "spiritual" sacrifices as a "spiritual" house (1 Pet. 2:5).

Let us not make the perilous mistake of transforming the practice of the church into a matter of letter. To do so will only invite spiritual weakness and defeat. As John W. Kennedy puts it,

> *The church of Jesus Christ is a living body, not a corpse. The imposition of a pattern has never yet made a church; not that pattern is unimportant . . . but the church is inseparable from spiritual life; it is not pattern alone . . . It can never be too strongly or too often emphasized that the imposition of a pattern, or simply the gathering of people together, does not bring the church into being. A church cannot be organized, it has to be born. (The Secret of His Purpose)*

At the same time, let us not focus upon the wine to the point of neglecting God's inspired wineskin. To have wine without the wineskin is a tragic mistake. When the wineskin is ignored, the Headship of Christ becomes nothing more than an abstract teaching without any concrete expression.

The tabernacle and the ark of the covenant go hand in hand. You cannot have the tabernacle without the ark. Neither can you have the ark without the tabernacle. Whether it is the tabernacle of Moses (Ex.25), the tabernacle of David (Acts 15:16), or the tabernacle (temple) of Solomon (1 Chron. 6:10), the tabernacle and the ark belong together. In the same way, Christ and the church always go together. The two must never be separated. Again, John W. Kennedy remarks,

> *It is remarkable to find so many devoted Christians who tend to look down upon any mention of church pattern or order. Life, they say, is all important, the pattern matters little. This attitude has largely succeeded in disembodying the church and thus curtailing the effectiveness of the Lord's testimony through His people. We have no more right to think that the pattern of the church is unimportant than we have to think that the pattern according to which we ourselves have been created does not matter . . . We should note that Paul deals with the principle first and the pattern afterwards. Unless there is a firm basis of spiritual life and understanding, the pattern can be worse than useless. (The Secret of His Purpose)*

Revisiting the Question at Hand

So what is the purpose of the church? The church exists to bear the testimony of Jesus. It is the family of God. It is the spiritual training-ground wherein the eternal purpose of God is worked out in human lives. It is the Divine building where every member is progressively transformed, reshaped, and fitted together to form the Lord's true temple.

The church is the habitat where the Lord's mind is obtained and expressed. It is the colonial outpost of the coming kingdom. It is the masterpiece of God.

The church is the spiritual "Bethany" where Jesus of Nazareth is received, obeyed, and adored in the midst of a rejecting world. It is the vessel in which the power of resurrection life is visibly displayed. It is the object of God's supreme affection and delight. It is the willing vehicle for Christ's manifested presence. It is the torch-bearer of the Divine testimony. It is the "one new man"—the new species—the "third race."

The church is the very fiancé of Jesus Christ. It is the new humanity. It is the lifestyle of the coming kingdom. It is the Christian's natural habitat. It is the spiritual environment where face-to-face encounters between the Bridegroom and His Bride take place. It is the living witness to the fullness of God's Son.

In short, whenever the church gathers together, its guiding and functioning principle is simply—*to be Christ* (1 Cor. 12:12).

CHAPTER 8

THE BODY OF CHRIST

In 1 Corinthians Paul writes, "For as the body is one, and hath many members, and all the members of that one body, being many, are one body: so also is Christ . . . Now ye are the Body of Christ, and members in particular" (1 Cor. 12:12,27).

The church is the Body of Jesus Christ. More specifically, the church is the Body of Christ in a given location. That is, the church *contains* all who are members of Christ's Body in a given location.

Therefore, if you are a member of the Body of Christ, you are part of the church in your locale. If you are not a member of the Body, you are not part of the church.

Life—The Only Basis for Oneness

Following this line of thought, Paul said to the church in Rome, "Him that is weak in the faith, receive . . . for God has received him . . . Wherefore receive ye one another, as Christ also received us to the glory of God" (Rom. 14:1,3; 15:7).

According to Paul, the church is made up of all whom God has received. And whomever God has received, we cannot refuse. Our receiving of others does not make them members of the church. We receive them because they are already members! Therefore, if God has received you, then you belong to the church. If God has received you, then I must receive you also.

The upshot of this is that all believers living in your vicinity should consider you a member of the household of God. And they should welcome fellowship with you. Why? Because you share the same life as that of every other Christian. All who share the indivisible life of Jesus Christ are part of the same church. The church contains all who are part of His Body.

Most Christians would agree with what I have just written. But many deny it in their practice. The trouble today is that scores of Christians have not made the Body of Christ the basis for their fellowship. They have either added or removed something from this basic requirement. Not a few modern "churches" have either exceeded or narrowed the Biblical basis for Christian unity—which is the Body of Christ. Allow me to unfold that a bit.

Suppose there is a group of Christians who meet regularly in your community. They call themselves "First Presbycharisbaptist Church." When you inquire about becoming a member, they hand you a "statement of faith" listing all their theological beliefs. Many of the doctrines that appear on this list go far beyond the essential foundations of the faith that mark all genuine Christians (such as the Deity of Jesus Christ, His saving work, His bodily resurrection, etc.).

As you continue to attend "First Presbycharisbaptist," you quickly discover that in order to be fully received by its members, you must hold to *their* view of spiritual gifts and eternal security. (Or perhaps *their* view of election and the second coming of Christ.) If you happen to disagree with them on one of these doctrinal points, you are made to feel that you would be happier attending elsewhere!

Do you see the problem with this? While "First Presbycharisbaptist" claims to be a church, they do not meet the Biblical requirement for a church. They have undercut the Biblical basis for fellowship, which is the Body of Christ *alone*! In the Lord's eyes, they are not a church. They are a *sect*.

Make no mistake about it. Nowhere does the Bible sanction us to divide from other believers on account of a doctrinal difference. On the contrary, God forbids any division on doctrinal grounds.

(Note that Romans 16:17 and Titus 3:9-11 do not refer to doctrinal error. They instead refer to people who use doctrine to polarize and embroil the church. These are those who use their own doctrinal beliefs to divide God's people.)

Again, if a person belongs to the Lord, then he is part of the church. And we must receive him into fellowship. If we demand anything beyond his acceptance of Christ before admitting him into fellowship, we are not a church. We are a sect. Again, all whom the Lord Jesus has received in a given locale make up the church.

The Problem of Sectarianism

Let us consider the meaning of the word *sect* as it appears in Scripture. The Greek word translated sect is *hairesis*. It is used nine times in the NT. It is translated "sect," "party," "faction," and "heresy."

A sect is a division or a schism. It refers to a body of people who have chosen to separate themselves from the larger whole to follow their own tenets. The classic example of the sin of sectarianism is found in 1 Corinthians 1:11-13. There Paul writes,

For it hath been declared unto me of you, my brethren, by them which are of the house of Chloe, that there are contentions among you. Now this I say, that every one of you saith, I am of Paul; and I of Apollos; and I of Cephas; and I of Christ. Is Christ divided? Was Paul crucified for you? Or were ye baptized in the name of Paul?

Note that in God's thought the Corinthian church included all the Christians who lived in the city of Corinth (1 Cor. 1:2). Yet some were drawing a circle around themselves that was smaller than the Body of Christ in Corinth. (Our carnal tendency to draw lines where they should not be drawn is prevalent in Christianity today.)

Instead of making the Body the basis of the church, some were making their favorite spiritual leader the basis for their fellowship. With loving severity, Paul rebuked such ones for their sectarian spirit. He condemned it as a work of the flesh (1 Cor. 3:3-4; Gal. 5:19-20; Jude 19).

If Paul's rebuke had not been heeded there would have arisen four different sects in Corinth. All of them claiming to be churches: "The church of Peter," "the church of Apollos," "the church of Paul," and "the church of Christ. (This latter group was saying, "We are the only ones who follow Christ. We do not need a worker like Paul, Peter, or Apollos to help us. We just need Jesus. We are *of Christ*.").

Anytime a group of Christians undercuts the Biblical basis for fellowship by excluding individuals that God has received—whether explicitly or implicitly—they are a sect. They may have a sign painted on their building that says "church." They may even be incorporated with "church status." But the Lord does not recognize them as a church! For they are sectarian.

In the language of Revelation, such groups have no lampstand. This, of course, does not mean that the members of a sect do not belong to the Body of Christ. But it does mean that the institution that they have constructed to pose as a church falls short of the spiritual reality.

Christians should not join sects. Sects are inherently divisive. God does not own them. To put it plainly, the only church we as believers can claim is the one that Jesus Christ began. It is the Body of Christ in local expression. Sadly, many modern Christians do not realize that what they are calling "their churches" are actually sects in the Lord's eyes.

While not a few Christians have *narrowed* the scope of the Body of Christ, others have *exceeded* it. In their attempt to be all-inclusive, these groups have sought oneness with unbelievers. This kind of oneness is foreign to the Bible. For only those whom Christ has received belong to His Body. And only they make up His church.

To receive unbelievers as family members is to turn the church into something earthly and to corrupt the true people of

God (1 Cor. 5:6; Gal. 2:4; 2 Tim. 3:6; 2 Pet 2:1; Jude 4,12). This of course does not mean that we should forbid unbelievers from attending the *gatherings* of the church (1 Cor. 14:23-24). But it does mean that we are not to receive them as our *brethren*. The oneness of the church, then, is limited to the Body of Christ. It cannot be extended beyond it.

Unity Through Organization

The church is severely divided in our day. The limbs of our Lord's Body have been butchered, fragmented, sliced and diced into denominations, movements, para-church organizations, and independent Bible studies.

Upon seeing the problem of sectarianism, some have proposed *organizational unity* as a solution. This brand of unity envisions all of the various strands of Christendom working together and relating to one another under the banner of a unified association. This kind of ecumenicism typically expresses itself at "the higher levels" only. The pastors of various churches meet together regularly, forming an association of ministers.

While such an expression of unity appears valid, it is wholly inadequate in God's eyes. It is nothing more than a human production. It only touches a segment of the Body of Christ (the clergy), and it fails to touch the root problem of sectarianism.

As long as Christians continue to separate from one another on the basis of a theological issue, a religious method, a worship style, or a spiritual practice, they are still meeting on sectarian ground.

This is the case even if different denominations have formed a federation of "churches" (sects). It remains true even if their ministers meet regularly for prayer. Such a display of unity is nothing more than holding hands over our fence! So long as men continue to maintain and justify their man-made fences, God cannot be satisfied.

While it is a noble step to accept those who are part of differing Christian traditions, we are foolish to boast about such a thing! The denominations are man-made divisions. They undermine Biblical principle. They fragment the Body of Christ.

For this reason, the early church knew no denominations. God's thought is for the "fence" to come down altogether! At the very least, He wishes that we jump over it and return to the only basis for Christian fellowship—the Body of Christ plus nothing! The Body of Christ minus nothing! The Body of Christ alone.

Unfortunately, a good number of believers today, especially a growing number of clergy, are not willing to touch that sore spot. It is far easier on our flesh to remain in close fellowship with those whose beliefs tally with our own. It is far more difficult to live with those who differ in doctrine, personality, worship style, spiritual practice, and the like.

While many Christians are willing to leave their comfort zones up to a point, most have a natural bent for presuming that God overlooks our compromise. The result is that the *good* becomes the enemy of the *best*. Many Christians have settled for a partial unity while simultaneously turning a deaf ear to God's *full* call for oneness.

Our day is similar to that of the kings of Israel who cleansed the temple but left the high places untouched. True oneness requires the power of the cross to work deeply in our lives. For this reason, Paul lovingly charged the church at Ephesus to be "longsuffering, forbearing one another *in love*, endeavoring to keep the unity of the Spirit in the bond of peace, for there is one Body . . ." (Eph. 4:2-4).

Such an exhortation makes little sense if those to whom Paul wrote divided into sects and only fellowshipped with each other when it was convenient and comfortable. On the contrary, the church that is envisioned in the NT did not divide into sects. It knew nothing of separating Christians according to denominational camps, Christian franchises, religious partisans, and spiritual tribal units!

Neither did it know anything about forming an association of clergy. Rather, every member of the Body of Christ in a given locale belonged to the same church. Not just in spirit, but in practical expression. Each believer saw all other believers as organs in the same Body. Bricks in the same building. Siblings in the same family. Soldiers in the same army.

In a word, the early Christians did not shake hands over the fence while professing to be one. They "lived together" in unreserved fellowship. And they refused to allow their flesh to erect such fences. John W. Kennedy well articulates the Lord's burden for unity when he says,

> *With the advent of the ecumenical movement, the hierarchy of a large section of organized Christianity has started to echo the cry of 'unity.' It does not seem to have been recognized, however, that union without communion is meaningless . . . Where there is not a heart that feels for one another, a crucifixion of self, and an entrance into 'Body consciousness' which is the product alone of regeneration and the continuous flow of the life and vitality of the Spirit, there can be no communion in any spiritual sense . . . A scattered pile of bricks is not a house, although they may be united in appearance; one brick looks very much like another. Similarly, a scattered company of regenerated people all claiming that they are one in Christ is not a church. They must be 'fitly framed together,' each one contributing his particular place in the spiritual building, and conscious of the bond of life and mutual responsibility which binds all of them together. The purpose of this unity is to form 'a habitation of God through the Spirit.' (The Secret of His Purpose)*

Unity Through Doctrine

Doctrinal unity is another idea that some have offered as a solution to mend the divisions in the church. Christians who endorse this type of unity talk much about the need for "doctrinal purity." But making doctrinal purity the basis for fellowship always ends up splintering the church further.

Those who stress doctrinal unity typically go about life extremely suspicious of their fellow brethren who are from other traditions. They do so under the guise of "defending the faith." While I believe that spiritual discernment is one of the most pressing needs among Christians today, it is fundamentally unbiblical and profoundly unchristian to go about scrutinizing our fellow brethren with a critical eye.

The Bible warns against those who are ruled by a prideful, fault-finding spirit. For this is the very spirit that marks the accuser of the brethren—the master divider of Christ's Body (Jude 16, NIV; Rev. 12:10)! If we make the Lord our sole pursuit, He will show us when falsehood is present. Yet if we are always seeking to smell the whiff of error in others, we will be sure to miss the Lord when He is speaking through one of His little ones.

Rather than actively looking to floodlight the misconceptions of other Christians, then, let us instead seek to find something of Christ whenever a brother or sister opens his or her mouth. Again, incorrect interpretations of the Bible is no grounds for dividing Christ's Body. If Jesus Christ has accepted you, I must also—despite how lacking in light you may be. And you must receive me on the same basis.

John W. Kennedy makes the point beautifully:

With man's passion to systematize the truth of Scripture there has come much light and blessing. No one must decry the devoted labors of the men of God down through the ages which have brought countless thousands a deeper appreciation of their inheritance in Christ. No human systematization of Divine truth, however, has any place for the church. To accept such is the way to stagnation, and is a prelude to further division among the people of God . . . When any assembly takes upon itself to teach a restricted code of doctrine as a church, then it has left the ground of the church entirely and has entered the domain of sectarianism. (The Secret of His Purpose)

Unity Through Organism

The Bible knows nothing of organizational or doctrinal unity. It only knows *organic unity*. The crucial issue regarding fellowship and oneness is that of *inward life*. The core question that ought to govern our fellowship is simply this: Has God received this person? Does the life of Christ reside in him? (Rom. 8:9; 2 Cor. 13:5). The indwelling life of Jesus Christ is the only requirement for the unity of the Spirit.

Certainly, those who have been born of the Spirit will live in a way that is consistent with this fact. It will also mean that they will hold to the *essential* doctrines regarding the Person of Jesus and His saving work. (See Eph. 4:3-7 for a listing of the seven principal factors necessary for spiritual unity.)

But it may also mean that they are not clear on certain spiritual things. Their personality may conflict with ours. Their worship style may be distasteful to us. They may be immature. They may be painfully eccentric. Their understanding of the Bible may be poverty stricken. Yet the fact that Christ dwells in them obligates us to receive them as family members. Not only "in word or in tongue, but in deed and in truth" (1 John 3:18).

Let No Man Be Deceived

Today the practical expression of the church's oneness is severely marred. God's people have splintered themselves into masses of disjointed, unconnected congregations all operating independently of one another. This grieves our Lord.

During the NT era, each church was completely unified. All of the believers in a locale lived as one family. If you and I lived in the city of Jerusalem, we belonged to the same church.

If I entertained thoughts of making my favorite apostle the basis of unity and ventured to meet with others of like mind to form "the church of Peter," I would be sternly corrected for my sectarian tendency. For to even profess that I belong to a man, a doctrine, or a method is both carnal and sectarian (1 Cor. 3:3-4).

Ironically, we make the same partisan distinctions without wincing when we say "I'm a Baptist," "I'm a Pentecostal," "I'm a Charismatic," "I'm a Calvinist," "I'm a Presbyterian," etc. (In fact, the word "denomination" literally means a name or designation for a class of things.)

We conveniently forget that Paul leveled a severe rebuke to the Corinthians when they began to denominate themselves in exactly the same way (1 Cor. 1:11-13). To be quite candid, the modern denominational system, which includes a large number of so-called non-denominational, post-denominational, and inter-denominational churches, is at variance with NT principle. Again, John W. Kennedy sums it up well:

> *Once we have known something of the vision of the Body, the spirit of 'my fellowship,' 'our group,' or differentiating between the Lord's people becomes abhorrent. To those who have tasted the fellowship of the church, sectarianism and the constrictions of denominationalism are intolerable. The basis of the church is the consciousness of the common life of the Spirit, and the Spirit gathers together on no other ground. (The Secret of His Purpose)*

The Scheme of the Enemy

There are few things that go right to the heart of the testimony of Jesus than the issue of fellowship. Consequently, Satan's chief scheme is directed at destroying the fellowship of the brethren. For it is by such division that he keeps the church in weakness.

As our Lord said, "A house divided against itself cannot stand." This being so, the forces of darkness seek every opportunity to cause us to divide. To cast suspicion on our fellow brethren. To judge them. To withdraw from them. Problems among brethren run far deeper than differences in temperament and opinion. The root is spiritual.

For the last 500 years, there has been an all-out assault by the enemy to destroy the Lord's testimony through divisions. Accordingly, we must be alive to the fact that the Lord's testimony is connected with our oneness. The only safeguard against divisiveness is to keep all that is natural in us firmly planted at the cross. This includes our opinions, natural preferences, likes and dislikes.

Unfortunately, many Christians have deluded themselves into welcoming division. Rational attempts to justify division always come down to an issue in ourselves that we are not willing to deal with. This is so even when our complaints against our brethren are legitimate.

Man, with his own fleshly mind, is quite clever at offering reasons why we cannot fellowship with certain brethren. How they fall short. How unworkable the situation is. How different they are from us. How unspiritual they may be, etc.

It is much easier on our flesh to give ground to such thoughts than to let God use the weaknesses of our brethren to deal with *us* in the essential areas of forbearance, longsuffering, and love.

It is in times of such difficulties that our belief in the oneness of the Body is brutally tested. It is here that God sorts out what is mere theory to us from what is real.

Summing it All Up

Christian oneness is as inclusive as the Body. Christians are to receive all who belong to His Body. Spiritual unity is neither organizational nor doctrinal. It is organic.

Fellowships that either undercut or exceed the scope of the Body are not Biblical churches. In God's thought, the church is one unified Body of His Son with local expressions throughout the world. Let us, therefore, cease from using the word "church" in a tribal sense where we equate it with Christian denominations, hierarchical structures of descending authority, program-driven institutions, and clergy-led enterprises.

The Body of Christ alone is the basis for the oneness of God's people. And the Lord has called us to have unclouded fellowship with all who are membered to it. So what God has joined together, let no man put asunder!

CHAPTER 9

THE CHURCH'S BOUNDARY

We have established that the *basis* of the church is the Body of Christ. Nothing more. Nothing less. But how does the church express its unity in a practical way? What is the *boundary* of the church?

By boundary, I am referring to the outward limit or border of the church. That is, where does a church start and where does it end in terms of geography? Such a question may appear at first glance to be academic and meaningless. But it is vital.

Today, we have a plethora of Christian congregations all claiming to be churches. These groups include denominations, house churches, cell groups, movements, non-denominational assemblies, gospel missions, and para-church organizations.

Can all of these groups justify their claim to be local expressions of the Body of Christ? Do they all have Scriptural grounds for being called "churches?" The pressing question to be addressed is: What justifies the existence of a church? Surprisingly, the answer to this question lies at the heart of how we Christians practically express our oneness in Christ.

As we shall see shortly, the Biblical basis for the existence of a church has to do with geography. The only Scriptural justification for dividing Christians into different churches is geographical distance. Nothing more. Nothing less.

Defining the Church

The Bible shows that the one Body of Christ expresses itself in many different places. These earthly expressions of the one Body are called "churches" (plural). We say that they are "local" because they are present in specifically defined geographical places ("locales").

In seeking to define the boundary of the church, let us look to the Savior's words in Matthew 18:15-20:

Moreover if thy brother shall trespass against thee, go and tell him his fault between thee and him alone: if he shall hear thee, thou hast gained thy brother. But if he will not hear thee, then take with thee one or two more, that in the mouth of two or three witnesses every word may be established. And if he shall neglect to hear them, tell it unto THE CHURCH: but if he neglect to hear THE CHURCH, let him be unto thee as an heathen man and a publican. Verily I say unto you, Whatsoever ye shall bind on earth shall be bound in heaven: and whatsoever ye shall loose on earth shall be loosed in heaven. Again I say unto you, That if two of you shall agree on earth as touching any thing that they shall ask, it shall be done for them of my Father which is in heaven. FOR WHERE TWO OR THREE ARE GATHERED TOGETHER IN MY NAME, THERE AM I IN THE MIDST OF THEM.

Here we find the essential definition of a church. It is a definition that is assumed throughout the rest of the NT. Upon careful reflection on this text, we discover that there are three characteristics of a church:

1) a plurality of people (*"two or three"*),
2) submission to the Headship of Christ (*"in my name"*), and
3) a corporate meeting in a specific place (*"where two or three are gathered together"*).

Whenever the believers in a given place gather together under the Headship of Christ, the Lord is present among them. Together they make up the church in its local expression.

This conclusion meshes perfectly with the description of the churches recorded in the book of Acts. Luke tells us that the apostles journeyed from region to region spreading the gospel message. When people in a given locale received the message, they immediately began to gather together. From that point on, they were collectively called "the church in" such and such a place (Acts 8:1; 11:22; 13:1, et al.).

The Meaning of Locale

Strikingly, everywhere the word "church" is used throughout the NT (excepting the passages which refer to the universal, heavenly church or a church in someone's house) it is identified by the *city*. By contrast, everywhere the word "churches" is used in the NT, it refers to the various churches that exist in a given *province* or *region*. Consider the following list:

The Church (of the City)	The Churches (of the Region)
The church of Antioch (of Syria)	*The churches of Asia*
Acts 13:1	*1 Cor. 16:19*
The church of Caesarea	*The churches of Cilicia*
Acts 18:22	*Acts 15:41*
The church of Cenchrea	*The churches of the Gentiles*
Rom. 16:1	*Rom. 16:4*
The church of Corinth	*The churches of Galatia*
1 Cor. 1:2	*1 Cor. 14:33*
The church of Ephesus	*The churches of Galilee*
Rev. 2:1	*Acts 9:31*
The church of Jerusalem	*The churches of Judea*
Acts 8:1	*Gal. 1:22*
The church of Laodicea	*The churches of Macedonia*
Rev. 3:14	*2 Cor. 8:1*
The church of Pergamos	*The churches of Samaria*
Rev. 2:12	*Acts 9:31*
The church of Philadelphia	*The churches of Syria*
Rev. 3:7	*Acts 15:41*
The church of Sardis	
Rev. 3:1	
The church of Smyrna	
Rev. 2:8	
The church of Thessalonica	
1 Thess. 1:1	
The church of Thyatira	
Rev. 2:18	

According to the Bible, the boundary of the church is the city. This is the reason why Paul commanded Titus to acknowledge elders in *every city* in the region of Crete (Titus 1:5). In like manner, Paul and Barnabas acknowledged elders in *every church* in the region of South Galatia (Acts 14:23).

We also learn from the book of Revelation that the Lord Jesus sees only *one* church in every city (Rev. 1:11-13,20). The declaration of Scripture, then, affirms that during NT times there existed only one church per city.

The Practical Expression of Our Oneness

At this point, let us inquire why the city is the boundary of the church. Was it just a passing cultural arrangement? Was it an aimless coincidence that presently lacks practical significance? Neither. The boundary of locale is directly tied to the practical expression of the oneness of the Body.

Many believers today have divided themselves into separate "churches" on the basis of a raft of issues. These issues are deemed to be legitimate grounds for Christian segregation. Yet when a given locale has an endless number of separate "churches" within its borders, the clear message sent to the world is that Jesus Christ is divided.

On the other hand, suppose that a group of believers refuses to divide for any reason other than geography? In other words, the only reason why they do not meet is because they live too far away from each other to gather feasibly.

These believers are devoted to one another in love. So much so that they refuse to separate on the basis of theology, spiritual leaders, worship style, prayer style, special ministry, race, socioeconomic status, etc. The only reason why they would divide is if they moved to another city. The unvarnished testimony sent to the world through such a people is that the Body of Christ is indeed one!

I have just described to you the outlook of the early church. Having one church per locale safeguards the unity of the Body of Christ and prevents sectarianism. When believers divide for reasons other than location, we, with Paul, are forced to raise the vexing question, "Is Christ divided?"

In his classic volume on the church and the work, Watchman Nee remarks,

> *Any division of the children of God other than geographical implies not merely a division of sphere, but a division of nature. Local division is the only division which does not touch the life of the church . . . It is our being in Christ that separates us from the world, and it is our being in a given locality that separates us from other believers. It is only when we reside in a different place from them that we belong to a different church. The only reason why I do not belong to the same church as other believers is because I do not live in the same place as they do. (The Normal Christian Church Life)*

The Danger of Legalism

Discussing locale is dangerous. Some who have seen this truth have become needlessly technical and legalistic concerning the exact specifications of a locale.

Given the enormous size and diversity of the Christian populace in many modern U.S. cities, some contextualization is necessary. Watchman Nee observes,

> *Questions will naturally arise concerning large cities such as London. Do they reckon one 'unity-locality' or more than one? London is clearly not a 'city' in the Scriptural sense of the term, and it cannot be regarded as a unit. Even people living in London talk about going 'into the city' or 'into town,' which reveals the fact that London and the city are*

not synonymous. The political and postal authorities, as well as the man on the street, regard London as more than one unit. They divide it respectively into boroughs and postal districts. What they regard as an administrative unit, we may well regard as a church unit. As to country places which would not technically be termed 'cities,' they may also be regarded as 'unit-localities.' It is said of our Lord, when on earth, that He went into the 'cities and villages' (Luke 13:22), from which we see that country-places, as well as towns, are considered to be separate units . . . Any place is qualified to be a unit for the founding of a church which is a place where people group together to live, a place with an independent name, and a place which is the smallest po- litical unit. Such a place is a Scriptural 'city' and is the boundary of the local church. (The Normal Christian Church Life)

Nee makes a valid point. Given the size of many modern cities, the geographical unit called "the community" better corresponds to the Biblical idea of a city. The church of Cenchrea (Rom. 16:1), for instance, was located only seven miles away from the church in Corinth. Cenchrea was a small town—a modern community if you will.

All technicalities aside, spiritual principle undeniably affirms that the only basis for separating Christians into different "churches" is geographical distance. Christians that divide from other believers on any other basis—be it a difference in race, worship style, social status, doctrinal interpretation, ministry emphasis, or spiritual leader—are sectarian (1 Cor. 1:11-13; 3:3-4)!

While this may sound shocking to some, I challenge my readers to find Biblical justification for separating the Body for any other reason than geography. (I am, of course, excepting unrepentant immorality and divisive activity which call for church discipline as outlined in Matt. 18:15-18; Rom. 16:17-18; 1 Cor. 5:1ff.; 2 Thess. 3:6-15; and Titus 3:10-11.)

Sectarianism in the Church

So the NT clearly sets forth the example of one church per locale. How is it, then, that there are hundreds of sects in the same city today all staking claim to be local churches? The answer ties directly into the subjects that we gave our attention to in Chapters 5 and 6. The reason for the endless divisions in the Body goes far deeper than our formal theologies reveal.

The present disorder began with the evolution of the clergy/laity class distinction. This distinction began to crystallize in the church around the late third century. The emergence of this hierarchical system, which violently ruptured the priesthood of all believers into a clergy class and a laity class, was the first major division known to the Body of Christ.

Various clergymen began to divide amongst themselves on theological matters. These events spawned a self-perpetuating ecclesiastical apparatus that later reproduced a raft of sects in every generation. The notable feature of these sects is that the people within them gather around their favorite leader (or doctrine) instead of around Christ.

Perhaps an analogy will help to illustrate this sad chain of events. Suppose that Bob, a so-called "layman," feels called to teach Scripture. In most modern basilica churches, he will have to "go into the ministry" and establish a church himself to fulfill his calling. Perish the thought of the pastor sharing his pulpit with a "layman" on a continuous basis—even if that "layman" has the gift of teaching! (See 1 Corinthians 14:26 for the folly in this mentality.)

After going through the proper institutional channels, Bob becomes a pastor. He begins a new church in his vicinity. In reality, Bob's "church" is nothing more than an extension of his own ministry. It is also an unneeded addition to the endless sects

eady exist in his community. All of which are competing
ach other to recruit members!

erein lies the root of the problem. The institutional church
Bob attended would not permit him to freely exercise his
teaching gift. Therefore, he saw no other alternative but to begin
a congregation of his own. (By the way, most modern churches
exist to give the pastor a platform by which to exercise his
teaching gift.)

The clergy/laity distinction is the seed-bed for the production
of endless schisms in the Body of Christ. When gifted people are
prevented from fulfilling their God-given callings, they feel
forced to begin their own churches. Even though God never
called them to do such a thing.

Such a tragic situation not only engenders countless sects, it
also forces thousands of gifted brethren to fulfill a job-de-
scription that the NT nowhere envisions: The single pastor!

This unbiblical office has tended toward the detriment of not
a few sincere Christians who have allowed themselves to come
within its wake. The clergy system is a faceless predator that
does not play favorites. It eats its young as well as all others who
agree to toil on its turf. In discussing the self-inflicted wounds
that are the product of this unbiblical system, Jon Zens candidly
remarks,

> *Like it or not, this 'clergy' role ends up requiring a virtual
> omni-competence from those behind the pulpit. 'Clergy' are
> paid to perform whatever is necessary to keep the religious
> machinery going, and the expectations are very high for
> those who wear the many hats this profession demands. The
> deadly problem with this unscriptural system is that it eats
> up those within its pale. Burn out, moral lapse, divorce,
> suicide are very high among the 'clergy.' Is it any wonder
> such repeated tragedies occur in light of what is expected of
> one person? Christ never intended anyone to fill such an
> ecclesiological role. ("The Clergy/Laity Distinction: A Help*

or a Hindrance to the Body of Christ?," Searching Together,
Vol. 23:4)

If Bob were a member of a first-century church, there would
have been no need for him to venture on his own to begin an
institution that God never sanctioned. As a member of a NT
church, Bob would have the freedom to function freely in his
teaching gift (see Chapter 1). Decisions would be made by
consensus. So Bob would have a voice in all of the church's
decisions (see Chapter 6).

Bob would only have left the church if he were an un-
speakably rebellious brother. If he moved to another city. If he
was ambitious to independently begin his own ministry. Or if
God called him to genuine apostolic work. (In which case the
church would send him out.)

Keep in mind that first-century apostles were not sent out to
build their own spiritual franchises. They established genuine
churches where there were none present. (For a fuller discussion
on the nature of apostolic ministry, see *Who is Your Covering?.*)

In sum, modern sectarianism finds it roots in the clergy/laity
class distinction. Diotrephes—whom John described as loving
to have "the preeminence"—is not alone in the history of men
who hunger for center stage in the church (3 John 9-10).
Lamentably, Diotrephes is still forbidding members of Christ's
Body from ministering in the Lord's house!

The Spirit's Cry for Oneness

The practical expression of our oneness is uppermost in
God's heart. Our Lord's final prayer was centered upon this very
point (John 17:11-26). Like the issue of church leadership,
expressing our oneness is inseparably connected to our submission to the Headship of Christ.

To use the body metaphor, if my hand and arm are both in
submission to my head, they will function in a unified manner.

There will be no schism among them. Division and disunity in the church uncover the fact that we are not holding fast to the Head (Col. 2:19). For when Jesus Christ is truly Head among a people, they fiercely refuse to divide from one another.

So *inwardly* the basis of the church is the Body of Christ. *Outwardly* the boundary of the church is the locale. Denominations (and a wide number of so-called non-denominational, post-denominational, and interdenominational churches) cannot be regarded as churches in the NT sense.

They all undercut the church's Scriptural boundary. The same is true with some "house churches" today. The locale, and not the house, is the boundary of the church.

Church Growth in the First Century

In the first century, when God raised up a church it invariably began in a house. When it grew, it multiplied into several homes. Yet each member saw himself as belonging to the same church. So while the church of Jerusalem met in various homes, it was collectively called "the church in Jerusalem."

It had the same founders. Its oversight was shared. And it assembled periodically as "the whole church" (Acts 15:1ff.). Churches that began small, like that of Corinth (Rom. 16:23), Rome (Rom. 16:5), Ephesus (1 Cor. 16:19), Laodicea (Col. 4:15-16), and Colosse (Phlm. 1-2), met in a single house until their numbers grew.

The church in Corinth that met at the house of Gaius was not a *separate* sub-church within the city of Corinth. Instead, the *entire* church in Corinth met in the home of Gaius (Rom. 16:23; 1 Cor. 14:23). The same holds true for the churches that began in the homes of Aquila and Priscilla, Nymphas, and Philemon.

While the house is the Scriptural setting for the church meeting (see Chapter 3), the *boundary* of the church is never the house. It is always the locale. An ongoing challenge for modern house churches is the danger of raising up several *independent* and *separate* house churches in the same community.

If a house church is not meeting upon the Biblical basis of one church per community, it will actually break the unity of the Body of Christ (just as the denominations do). The existence of multiple house churches in the same locale that have no fellowship with one another is a departure from Divine principle. It was never God's thought that churches existing in the same vicinity carve out separate identities.

The Greek word translated "church" in the NT is *ekklesia*. And it literally means "a physical gathering." Robert Banks explains:

> *The term 'ekklesia' consistently refers to actual gatherings of Christians as such, or to Christians in a local area conceived or defined as a regularly assembling community. This means that 'church' has a distinctly dynamic rather than static character. It is a regular occurrence rather than an ongoing reality. The word does not describe all the Christians who live in a particular community who do not gather. (Paul's Idea of Community)*

Watchman Nee echoes the same thought saying,

> *It is essential that there be a physical gathering together of believers. It is not enough that they be present 'in the spirit,' they must also be present 'in the flesh.' Now a church is composed of all 'the called-out ones assembled' in one place for worship, prayer, fellowship, and ministry. This assembling together is absolutely essential to the life of a church. Without it there may be believers scattered throughout the area, but there is really no church. (The Normal Christian Church Life)*

All in all, churches that meet in homes must see themselves as part of the one Body of Christ in their locales rather than as separate and independent entities. God desires that the invisible unity of the church be expressed in a visible way.

Simply stated, the NT only knows one church in the locale. For the early Christians, this was not a doctrine. It was taken for granted. To their minds, the thought of having two churches in the same locale would be as unthinkable (to our minds) as having two mayors in the same city. The early Christians understood Christian oneness. So "locale" was not a defined doctrine for them.

But be clear. It was never God's thought that the Body of Christ be turned into the denominational morass that exists today. Nor was it His thought for Christians to be divided into independent house churches in the same locale that have nothing to do with one another.

Indeed, it is not enough for us to leave the sects. Sectarianism must leave us! Our endorsement of the denominations and other factions betrays our alleged belief that the Body of Christ is one.

God's Reaction to the Present Division

So where does this leave us? What is the remedy for the endless divisions in the Body? It is certainly not found in the formation of an association of sects or ministers who hold hands over the fence. Institutional ecumenicism is not God's answer. Neither is the intangible idea that one day God will destroy every existing sect.

The Lord's reaction to the present disorder is to raise up a *representative company* of believers who will respond to the Spirit's cry for genuine unity. His is a charge to leave the man-made sects and to meet freshly upon the first-century basis of the church.

Those who gather on this basis do not claim to be anyone special. They are simply seeking to be faithful to the NT vision of Jesus Christ and His church. A vision that has powerfully captured their hearts. They receive all whom God has received, whether they meet in sects or not. They include all believers living in their locales. They welcome unreserved fellowship with any and all who wish to gather with them.

At the same time, they cannot endorse a system that smacks square in the face of NT revelation. They do not deny the fact that God has used (and still uses) the denominations as best He can. For God often uses that which He does not approve.

At the same time, they cannot support the denominational system. Nor can they join the sects. They simply cannot settle for anything less than what corresponds to God's *full* thought for His Son's Body. Gene Edwards sums up the spirit of those believers who hold such a testimony saying,

> *Christendom has, by and large, for the last 1700 years, been part of the world system, and it has been structured like all the secular institutions of the earth. Yet there have always been Christians in every age who would not conform to this tradition . . . We take our place abreast of those who were determined to know nothing but Christ; to march with those little bands who were seeking a full experience of the Body of Christ . . . the experience of the church! . . . With malice toward none and charity toward all, we have stepped outside of the traditional church to stand with the organic expression of the Body of Christ. (Climb the Highest Mountain)*

Stephen Kaung shares the same burden:

> *We so gather because we believe in the oneness of the Body of Christ—one Head, one Body. We are called into one Body. We are grieved—we have wept—over the divisions among God's people. We want to return to the simple*

ground of the unity of the Body of Christ. People may say,
'You separate yourself; you cause division . . . ' But God
knows our heart. We come out of divisions to return to unity.
That's what we are doing. Therefore, on the one hand, we
hold fast the Head; on the other hand, we open our heart
and arms to all our brothers and sisters all over the world.
No matter what background you are from, what special
teaching you have, or what experience you have, brothers
and sisters, if you are the Lord's, you belong to us and we
belong to you. This is why we so gather. You may reject us,
but we cannot reject you because we believe in the oneness
of the Body of Christ . . . We come out of sects not to be
sectarian, but to be delivered from the spirit of sectarianism.
(Why Do We So Gather?)

Peacefully and quietly, without pride or boast, these believers seek to maintain the pure and simple testimony that Jesus
Christ is Head and that His Body is one. Such are the lampstands
that stand before the Lord. They are the small and often unnoticed vessels for the recovery of His testimony. They stand for
the outworking of His eternal purpose.

May you count yourself worthy to stand with them!

CHAPTER 10

THE APOSTOLIC TRADITION

Thomas F. Torrance once said the following:

There can be no doubt that every one of the great churches of the Reformation has developed its own masterful tradition, and that tradition today exercises massive influence not only over its way of interpreting the Bible and formulating its doctrine, but over the whole shape and direction of its life. Those who shut their eyes to this fact are precisely those who are most enslaved to the dominant power of tradition just because it has become an unconscious canon and norm of their thinking. It is high time we asked again whether the Word of God really does have free course among us and whether it is not after all bound and fettered by the traditions of men. The tragedy, apparently, is that the very structures of our churches represent the fossilization of traditions that have grown up by practice and procedure, and they have become so hardened in self-justification that even the Word of God can hardly crack them open. (Quoted in Verdict, Vol. 3, No. 4, Oct. 1980)

The Tradition of the Apostles

Virtually every segment of the Christian church operates on the basis of some historical tradition handed down to them by their spiritual forefathers. For some denominations, these traditions comprise the very fabric that holds them together. They define the church's purpose through statements of faith, confessions, creeds, and canons.

In response to this tendency, many neo-denominations (Vineyard, Calvary Chapel, etc.) hold anything that smacks of the word "tradition" to be anathema. They have distanced themselves from any practice remotely routine or binding. (Interestingly, most churches that claim to be free from the influence of tradition have merely created their own!)

The irony of these two tendencies lies here. Much attention has been given to the calcified, ecclesiastical traditions of men. But very little has been given to the Divine tradition passed on by the apostles of Jesus Christ.

Consider the following passages that allude to this tradition:

Therefore I urge you to IMITATE ME . . . my way of life in Christ Jesus, which agrees with WHAT I TEACH EVERY-WHERE IN EVERY CHURCH. (1 Cor. 4:16-17, NIV)

I praise you because you remember me in everything, and HOLD FIRMLY TO THE TRADITIONS JUST AS I DE-LIVERED THEM TO YOU. (1 Cor. 11:2, NASB)

But if one is inclined to be contentious, WE HAVE NO OTHER PRACTICE, NOR HAVE THE CHURCHES OF GOD. (1 Cor. 11:16, NASB)

For God is not a God of confusion but of peace, AS IN ALL THE CHURCHES OF THE SAINTS. (1 Cor. 14:33, NASB)

Brethren, join in following my example, and observe those who walk ACCORDING TO THE PATTERN YOU HAVE IN US. (Phil. 3:17, NASB)

The things you have learned and received and heard AND SEEN IN ME, PRACTICE THESE THINGS, and the God of peace shall be with you. (Phil. 4:9, NASB)

So then, brethren, stand firm AND HOLD TO THE TRA-DITIONS WHICH YOU WERE TAUGHT, whether by word of mouth or by letter from us. (2 Thess. 2:15, NASB)

Now WE COMMAND YOU BRETHREN, in the name of our Lord Jesus Christ, that you keep aloof from every brother who leads an unruly life and NOT ACCORDING TO THE TRADITION WHICH YOU RECEIVED FROM US. (2 Thess. 3:6, NASB)

For you yourselves know how YOU OUGHT TO FOLLOW OUR EXAMPLE . . . (2 Thess. 3:7, NASB)

. . . But in order TO OFFER OURSELVES AS A MODEL FOR YOU, THAT YOU MIGHT FOLLOW OUR EXAMPLE. (2 Thess. 3:9, NASB)

What the Apostolic Tradition is Not

The tradition of the apostles is not a formal codified set of prescribed rules that the apostles created. Neither is it a detailed manual for church practice. (The truth is, no such manual exists. Even though some have tried to construct such a manual today!)

The Bible is rather scanty concerning the details of the early church's practice. The reason for this is quite simple. If such a detailed explanation existed, there would be no place for the guidance of the Holy Spirit. The Law would replace the Spirit. The wineskin would overshadow the wine. And the church would drift into a modern replica of ancient Judaism—caught in the legalistic mold of a mechanical adherence to forms.

Technical correctness and outward conformity to a prescribed form of church order, ritual, or liturgy has never been God's thought. Such cold formalism will only yield death. It will also smother the organic life of the Body of Christ.

The church is a living organism. By it, the Spirit of God works out God's eternal purpose in fresh ways. The church is a corporate, living entity. It is that which comes *out of* Christ. As Eve came out of Adam's side, so the church has its origin in the Heavenly Man (compare Gen. 2:21-23 with Eph. 5:23-32). Because Christ is alive, the church is also alive.

If we understand that the church is not only built *by* Christ, but *out of* Christ, we will be safeguarded from turning the church into a method or a technique. Not a few Christians have made the NT a system of church order. Whenever this is done, the church becomes a method and the Lord Jesus is altogether lost.

Church practice must be kept in vital relation to the living Head. If the Body severs itself from its Head, it dies. Put differently, the life of the Body resides in the Head. And a body divorced from its head is a corpse. The church, therefore, has no existence apart from Jesus Christ. Neither does it have any existence apart from God's purpose.

The practice of the church is bound up with something far higher than a *pro forma* adherence to a prescribed pattern. Even if that pattern happens to be based in the NT. In the words of T. Austin-Sparks,

> *The ministry of the Holy Spirit has ever been to reveal Jesus Christ, and revealing Him, to conform everything to Him. No human genius can do this. We cannot obtain anything in our NT as the result of human study, research, or reason. It is all the Holy Spirit's revelation of Jesus Christ. Ours is to seek continually to see Him by the Spirit, and we shall know that He—not a paper-pattern—is the Pattern, the Order, the Form. It is all a Person who is the sum of all purpose and ways . . . Everything [in the early church] then was the free and spontaneous movement of the Holy Spirit, and He did it in full view of the Pattern—God's Son. (Words of Wisdom and Revelation)*

The Spirit of God will never lead us into a dead orthodoxy based upon external forms. Nor will He ever divorce the Body from its living Head. Rather, the Spirit always works according to defined spiritual principles.

A spiritual principle is simply a tendency that is part of God's nature. God is a Divine Person. So He has certain tendencies that reflect His Divine nature. When these tendencies are evidenced in Scripture, we call them principles. And it is these spiritual principles (or Divine tendencies) that constitute the underpinnings of the apostolic tradition.

Testifying from personal experience T. Austin-Sparks explains,

> *God's way and law of fulness is that of organic life. In the Divine order, life produces its own organism, whether it be vegetable, animal, human, or spiritual. This means that everything comes from the inside. Function, order, and fruit issue from this law of life within. It was solely on this principle that what we have in the NT came into being. Organized Christianity has entirely reversed this order . . . Thus, having set aside all the former system of organized Christianity, we committed ourselves to the principle of the organic. No 'order' was 'set up,' no officers or ministries were appointed. We left it with the Lord to make manifest by 'gift' and anointing who were chosen of Him for oversight and ministry. The one-man ministry has never emerged. The 'overseers' have never been chosen by vote or selection, and certainly not by the expressed desire of any leader. No committees or official bodies have ever existed in any part of the work. Things in the main have issued from prayer. (Words of Wisdom and Revelation)*

Recovering the Place of Tradition

The NT word for tradition is the Greek word *paradosis*. It denotes that which is handed down. So what is the apostolic tradition? First, it contains the stories of Jesus. Stories about His earthly life and ministry. (These are contained in the Gospels.) Second, it includes the commands and practices of the apostles that were passed on to all the churches (1 Cor. 11:23ff.; 15:1-3; 2 Pet. 3:1-2).

The apostolic tradition represents the normative beliefs and practices of the early church. So when Paul made reference to the universal practice of all the churches, he was appealing to the apostolic tradition (1 Cor. 4:16-17; 11:16; 14:33-38).

These were not practices that Paul merely *described.* They were *prescribed* for each and every church. Eminent NT scholar F.F. Bruce observes,

> *When we examine Paul's references to the tradition of Christ, it appears to have comprised three main elements: (a) a summary of the Christian message, expressed as a confession of faith, with special emphasis on the death and resurrection of Christ; (b) various deeds and words of Christ; (c) ethical procedural rules for Christians . . . What was derived from the earthly Jesus and was transmitted through the apostles was at the same time continuously validated by the exalted Lord through His Spirit in the apostles, so that revelation and apostolic tradition are but two sides of the one coin . . . as the ever-living Christ He maintains and authenticates the tradition throughout the apostolic age until it ceases to be oral tradition and becomes Holy Scripture. Tradition is thus one way the Risen Lord imparts His revelation through the Spirit. (Tradition: Old and New)*

The tradition of the apostles is contained within Scripture. Thus the notion held by some Catholic and Orthodox theologians that there exists a mysterious body of authoritative and infallible tradition outside of the Bible is untenable.

Rather, the apostolic tradition is the embodiment of those spiritual principles and organic practices that the apostles modeled in every church during the first century. It is these principles, methods, and lines of working that constitute the wineskin that God has formed to preserve His new wine.

If our church practice is derived from life, it will be in harmony with the apostolic tradition. This is because the teachings of the apostles are rightly expressed through their practices. Therefore, what is written in the NT concerning how the apostles conducted themselves is not to be viewed as irrelevant history. It is to be considered with great care.

Some may argue that if we are rightly following the Holy Spirit's rule there is no need to give our attention to first-century practices. However, this argument ignores the fact that we are fallible creatures who easily confuse the Spirit's guidance with our own. Accordingly, we must realize that in order for us to discover the source of our leading, our church practice must have a Biblical basis.

To ignore apostolic traditions is to put us in the dangerous position of unknowingly substituting our misguided feelings and unfounded thoughts for the Spirit's leading. The NT, then, is to be our standard for faith and practice. Both for individual conduct as well as for corporate life. Watchman Nee points out,

If we would understand the will of God concerning His church, then we must not look to see how He led His people last year, or ten years ago, or a hundred years ago, but we must return to the beginning, to the 'genesis' of the church, to see what He said and did then. It is there we find the highest expression of His will. Acts is the 'genesis' of the church's history, and the church in the time of Paul is the 'genesis' of the Spirit's work. Conditions in the church today are vastly different from what they were then, but these present conditions could never be our example, or our authoritative guide; we must return to the 'beginning.' Only what God has set forth as our example in the beginning is the eternal will of God. It is the Divine standard and our pattern for all time. . . Circumstances may differ and cases may differ, but in principle the Will and Ways of God are just the same today as they were in the book of Acts. (The Normal Christian Church Life)

G.H. Lang draws the same inescapable conclusion saying,

Nor is there a need, nor can there be hope, of improving upon the Lord's orderings. He knew perfectly the purposes which His church was to serve in the earth, and knew fully the conditions amidst which it must work; and He instituted through His apostles the very best arrangements and methods for doing the intended work in the given conditions. To assume otherwise is to impute folly to God. It is a fallacy that conditions alter essentially, or indeed at all, in relation to the business of the church of God. God changes not; His claims upon and principles of conduct for mankind alter not; the sinfulness and rebellion of the natural man abide undiminished; and, for the purpose in view, racial and religious differences, or a local veneer of mental education or of civilization, matter nothing . . . As, then, all the essential factors abide as they were in the apostolic times, the apostolic plan of church life and of Christian service will be, and has been, found to be as Divinely suited to this age as to that; indeed, Scripturally speaking, it is but one age. (The Churches of God)

The NT presents the church in its purest form. It shows us what the church was like before it was tainted by the defiling hand of man. Therefore, it is in the NT that we must look to discern the Spirit's leading for us today. Both on an individual as well as on a corporate plane.

If we ignore Scripture on these points, we will make the perilous mistake of creating a church after our image. As Stephen Kaung says,

People believe that the Word of God shows them how to live individually before God, but they think that insofar as their corporate life is concerned, God says, 'It's up to you; do whatever you like.' And that's what we find today in Christianity; there is no guiding principle as to our corporate life—everyone does what is right in his own eyes. But dear brothers and sisters, we are saved individually, but we are called corporately . . . there is as much teaching and example in the Word of God that governs our corporate life as there is our personal life. (Who Are We?)

Starting at the Right End

It must be emphasized that before we can truly understand anything meaningful about the church, we must first be captured by a consuming revelation of the Person for whom it exists. Therefore, we must always begin with the Lord Jesus. We must always start with Him.

If we start out with the church, instead of with the One for whom it lives, we will end up with something quite distorted. Russell Lipton rightly remarks,

The church is so important! Yet her significance fades away compared to the glory of our Christ Himself. We face grave dangers when we 'major' on the church and especially on its 'structure.' We should major on the Lord and minor on the church . . . at most . . . If Christ is not exalted, we are building on sand, using wood, hay, and stubble as materials. All will be burned up. Whenever Christians, throughout the age, have built on a foundation other than Christ, the storms have come and living churches have fallen into spiritual death. (Does the Church Matter?)

Again, the church is not an end in itself. Scripture gives the greatest attention to the Person and Work of the Lord Jesus Christ as the center and circumference of the full purpose of God. Its primary attention is fastened upon the weighty matters of His Lordship, His kingdom, His victorious triumph, His glorious character, His life in the believers, His second coming, and His universal rule. It is all about Him!

So the stress of Scripture is upon the wine (Christ in the Spirit). Nevertheless, God's wine needs a wineskin (church order) to contain and pour it forth. If we fail to pay attention to

the wineskin that is recorded in the NT, the wine of God's life
will leak out or become spoiled.

The wineskin has been given for the practical outworking of
our glorious inheritance in Christ. Its purpose is simple: To
contain and express the riches of His glory. Put differently, the
Lord has given us truth regarding the *organism* of the church as
well as its *order*. In this vein, Watchman Nee explains,

> *The danger, with those who know little about life and reality,
> is to emphasize mere outward correctness: but with those to
> whom life and reality are a matter of supreme importance,
> the temptation is to throw away the Divine pattern of things,
> thinking it legal and technical . . . Of course, the mere
> observance of outward forms of service has no spiritual
> value whatever. All spiritual truths, whether pertaining to
> the inner or outer life, are liable to be legalized. Everything
> that is of God—whether outward or inward—if in the Spirit
> is life, if in the letter it is death. So the question is not, Is it
> outward or inward? but, Is it in the Spirit or in the letter?
> 'The letter killeth, but the Spirit giveth life . . . ' We seek to
> follow the leading of God's Spirit, but at the same time we
> seek to pay attention to the examples shown us in His Word
> . . . God has revealed His Will, not only by giving orders, but
> by having certain things done in His church, so that in all
> ages to come others might simply look at the pattern and
> know His Will . . . Precepts have their place, but examples
> have no less important a place, though obviously conformity
> to the Divine pattern in outward things is mere formality if
> there is no correspondence in inner life. (The Normal
> Christian Church Life)*

The Place of Organism and Order in the Church

While the church is first and foremost an organism, it does
have order. Like leadership, order *is*. Whenever God's people
gather together, a certain order or form will eventually emerge.

The form can be liberating or oppressive. Scriptural or un-scriptural. Helpful or harmful. But it always exists. In the words of Howard Snyder,

> *All life must have form. Life without form is sick and dies; it perishes because it cannot sustain itself. That is the way it is with all life, whether human, spiritual, or botanical, for God in His creation is consistent. (The Community of the King)*

Church order, therefore, is both inevitable and important. An apt example of this truth is found in our Lord's scathing rebuke of the scribes and Pharisees. In Matthew 23, we find the Master repudiating their rabbinical tradition. He denounces their unjustified obsession with external correctness. He lays bare their bondage to outward forms.

Jesus upbraids the scribes and Pharisees for shifting the Divine priorities saying, "For you make clean the outside of the cup and of the platter, but within they are full of extortion and excess . . . For you tithe mint and dill and cummin, and have neglected the weightier provisions of the law: justice and mercy and faithfulness."

Here the Lord scolds these religious leaders for stressing outward correctness to the neglect of inward purity. But notice that He did not discount the importance of the outward matters. He went on to say, "These ye ought to have done, *and not to have left the other undone*" (Matt. 23:23). So God's highest value rests upon inward spiritual reality (organism). But He does not ignore its outward expression (order).

The fact is that there is both order and life—form and function—in the church of Jesus Christ. A.W. Tozer insightfully redresses the delicate balance between the two saying,

> *Some will have no organization at all, and of course the results are confusion and disorder, and these can never help mankind or bring glory to the Lord. Others substitute*

organization for life, and while having a name to live they are dead. Still others become so enamored with rule and regulations that they multiply them beyond all reason, and soon the spontaneity is smothered within the church and the life is squeezed out of it. (God Tells the Man Who Cares)

Where Modern Evangelicalism Has Gone Wrong

Many modern evangelicals have embraced the benighted idea that only those things that are "explicitly commanded" in Scripture are binding. Everything else can be safely ignored. Ironically, most who espouse this idea deny it in their practice.

They rigorously defend the importance of having the Lord's Supper on a regular basis, the necessity of baptizing new converts, and the importance of assembling together on a weekly basis. Yet none of these practices is explicitly commanded in Scripture!

Equally problematic is the notion that only the "principles" of the early church are to be heeded while its "practices" are irrelevant and antiquated. This idea has deluded many Christians into embracing a raft of humanly-devised practices that violate spiritual principles. For example, salaried clergy, single pastors, pulpit-pew styled services in basilica-like spaces, denominations, etc. are all at odds with spiritual principle!

The truth lies here. Normative apostolic *commands* are binding for the modern church. But the normative apostolic *practices* are as well. By normative, I mean those practices that assume the following characteristics: 1) They were established by the apostles in *all* the primitive churches; 2) They are life-bound rather than culture-bound; 3) They contain a spiritual subtext.

Such practices are not purely narrative. They also carry prescriptive force. This means that they reflect the unchanging nature of God Himself. And they naturally emerge whenever God's people live by Divine life together.

The book of Acts and Paul's epistles are awash with references to the apostolic tradition. These Spirit-inspired writings present both basic spiritual principle as well as local application. In Acts, Luke uses narrative to teach theological truth. His writing merges principle and practice together.

Principle and practice are interwoven throughout Paul's epistles as well. In 1 Corinthians 4:17, Paul declares how he *taught* his *ways* "everywhere" in "every church." To Paul's mind, doctrine and duty—belief and behavior—life and practice—are inseparable.

Consequently, that which is included in the apostolic tradition is normative practice for all churches yesterday and today. The exhortation of Paul to "hold firmly to the traditions just as I delivered them to you"—practice what "you have learned and received and heard and seen in me" are the considerations that should guide us in our church life.

Intersecting Tradition and Teaching

Adhering to the apostolic tradition does not mean reenacting the events of the first-century church. If so, we would have to hold our meetings in an upper chamber with many lights (Acts 20:8). We would have to cast lots to appoint our leaders (Acts 1:26). We would have to climb upon roof-tops at the hour of prayer (Acts 10:9). Not to mention having to speak and dress like all first-century believers did, in sandals and togas!

Instead, observing apostolic traditions means following what was *theologically* and *spiritually* significant in the experience of the early church. The apostolic tradition represents the balance between *reenacting* the specific actions of the first-century church and *ignoring* them.

The truth is that there are numerous practices of the early church that are normative for us today. These practices are not culturally conditioned. They are rather tied to our faith and obedience. And they are deeply rooted in Biblical theology. Such practices give practical expression to the spiritual realities that are in Jesus Christ. They are the Divine *means* for expressing the Divine *purpose*. Russell Lipton puts it this way:

> *Doctrine informs the heart and changes the inner man.*
> *Practice enables us to embody doctrine and turn doctrine*
> *into testimony. While practices did evolve and shift to some*
> *degree throughout the decades of the early church, we have*
> *no warrant from Scripture to minimize or evade NT prac-*
> *tices and introduce our own. At most, we may experiment*
> *with fresh forms that are clearly, unmistakably and de-*
> *fensibly tied to those first practices. But if we are wise, we*
> *will live out the practices of the apostles as well as their*
> *doctrine. ("Devotion to Practices," unpublished article)*

Apostolic tradition incarnates apostolic teaching. It gives shape to spiritual reality. Open participatory church meetings are solidly based upon the well-established doctrine of the priesthood of all believers (see Chapter 1). Observance of the Lord's Supper as the communion of the church is built upon the centrality of Jesus Christ and the covenantal relationship of the believing community (see Chapter 2).

House church meetings rest squarely upon the fact that the church is a face-to-face community. It is a close-knit, extended family that engages in mutual sharing and edification (see Chapter 3). Plural oversight and decision-making by consensus are firmly grounded in the practical operation of the functioning Headship of Christ (see Chapter 6).

A fully functioning priesthood is the Divine means for expressing the eternal purpose (Chapter 7). Finally, the Scriptural basis of one church per locale is rooted in the teaching of the oneness of the Body of Christ (see Chapters 8 and 9).

Granted, there are other first-century practices beyond the ones just mentioned. Church planting by itinerant apostolic workers; gospel preaching; acts of mercy and social justice; the baptizing of new converts; the training and support of apostolic workers, et al. are some examples.

In short, every principle that is a part of the apostles' tradition is vitally connected to an unshakeable Scriptural teaching. Apostolic practice represents the God-ordained means of expressing His life. The function and form of the church are complimentary notions in Scripture.

The form of the church should always follow the function of the church. Yet the church's form should not be ignored. Correct form does not ensure nor guarantee life. But if a church possesses life, it will embrace those forms that will facilitate the building up of the Body. As one writer remarks,

All church structure (including the structure of authority) must come forth spontaneously from 'life.' The river ('life') makes its own riverbed (structure). We cannot make the riverbed (structure) and then invite the river ('life') to come through our construction. Rather, the river moves and as it does it makes its own riverbed to flow through. So the life of the Spirit in the assembly will form its own structure. Thus all NT structure is flexible (moves with life) and not rigid (Matt. 9:14-17). However, the basic structure of the church is set forth in the Scriptures and should be studied and restudied so as to check the structure being formed. The Spirit does not bring structures that are in opposition to the Word. (Rudy Ray, "Authority in the Local Church," Searching Together, Vol. 13:1)

When the Holy Spirit has His sovereign way in birthing a church, it will spontaneously gather in a Biblical fashion. The church will organically fulfill the apostolic tradition. As Paul said, those who follow the Spirit (the spiritual) will adhere to the apostolic tradition regarding church order (1 Cor. 14:37).

Regrettably, the tradition of the apostles has been largely ignored today. It has been viewed as irrelevant in the eyes of many modern Christians. The *apostolic* tradition has been buried under a mountain of *human* tradition!

Multitudes of church leaders today have opted to regard their own ideas of "doing church" as wiser, more expedient, and more successful than what is found in the NT. The tragedy of this mistaken conclusion is manifold. When Divine tendencies are replaced with man-officiated programs and schemes, God's ordained purpose for the *ekklesia* is crippled at best. It is crushed at worst.

The Importance of the Apostolic Tradition

Paul responded with unusual sharpness toward those who departed from the apostolic tradition saying,

> *Did the Word of God originate with you? Or are you the only people who it has reached? If anybody thinks he is a prophet or spiritually gifted, let him acknowledge that what I am writing to you is the Lord's command. If he ignores this, he himself will be ignored. (1 Cor. 14:36-38, NIV)*

It would do us well to remember that Divine truth is understood both by precept and example. This is the case all throughout Scripture. So to disregard the organic *principles* and *examples* of Scripture is to betray the *teachings* of Scripture.

Surprisingly, a church may abandon the apostolic tradition in lieu of its own self-constructed form and still have God's blessing in some measure. This has caused not a few Christians to conclude that NT example isn't important. Yet we mustn't be deceived into thinking that God's *blessing* equals His *approval*.

The history of Israel teaches us that God can still bless a people who disregard His ways for their own. Throughout Israel's wilderness journeys, God met His people's needs. This despite the fact that He was continually angry with them. When the children of Israel clamored for a king in their rebellion against the Divine will, the Lord condescended to their carnal desire (1 Sam. 8:1ff.). And he continued to bless them despite their disobedience.

But tragic consequences followed their self-motivated decision (1 Sam. 8:11-18). The nation lost its freedom under a raft of evil monarchs. And it suffered a series of Divine judgments. There is a sad parallel between the condition of Israel and many of God's people today who have opted for an earth-tied, man-managed religious system. It bears repeating: God's blessing does not equate His approval.

The Challenge of Unfeigned Obedience

Because He is mercy, the Lord will bless any group of people if He can find some ground to do so. But when they choose their own ways in place of His, they severely limit His hand. The Lord is very jealous over His house (see Rev. 1-3). And He is not satisfied with our human arrangements when it comes to the church.

Oh, how quickly we forget that the church belongs to God and not to us! Dear reader, be clear that it is part of our fallen nature to follow our own ideas regarding church practice. To enshrine our own traditions. To canonize our own personal preferences. To institutionalize what fits our own ideas of success rather than to follow what the apostles have handed down to us.

So I ask you: Where do you get the right to change NT principle? What basis do you have to ignore the tradition of the apostles in preference for your own? What authority do you have to replace plural oversight with hierarchical forms of government? Where do you get the right to support a single pastor system? What exegetical basis do you have to replace open participatory meetings with program-based, man-officiated services that foster passivity and suppress functioning? What grounds do you have for dividing yourself from other members of His Body? What right do you have to tamper with what the Lord has prescribed for His own house!?

The words of the honorable theologian John Stott come to mind:

The hallmark of an authentic evangelicalism is not the uncritical repetition of old traditions, but the willingness to submit every tradition, however ancient, to fresh Biblical scrutiny and, if necessary, reform." ("Basic Stott," Christianity Today, Jan. 8, 1996)

I press the question directly: If your church practices come in direct conflict with NT revelation, are you willing to adjust them?

Let God Build His House

An unmistakable theme of the Bible is that God leaves nothing for man to decide when it comes to His house. It is Christ's House that He is building in His Way. He is the God of the *end* as well as the God of the *means*. All must be of Him, through Him, and to Him if it will have any lasting value. Again, the church comes out of Christ. How dare we try to reform it into our own image!

Consequently, it is not the size of the building that is God's chief concern. It is what the building is composed of (1 Cor. 3:9-15). In the Lord's eyes, *how* we build and *what* we build with are more important than the size and appearance of the building.

"Unless *the Lord* builds the house," declares the Psalmist, "they labor in vain that build it" (Ps. 127:1). God alone is the Master "architect and builder" (Heb. 11:10). Especially when it comes to His own dwelling place! In God's work, the governing principle is always, "Lord . . . all that we have accomplished you have done for us" (Isa. 26:12, NIV).

The tragic story of King David's presumptuous act of placing the ark of the Lord upon a wooden cart is the summary witness that God's work must be done His way (2 Sam. 6:1-7). The humanly-devised scheme of placing the holy ark upon a cart appeals to modern pragmatic ears. Yet the idea was borrowed from the heathen Philistines. And it violated the plain instruction of Jehovah (Exod. 25:12-16; Num. 4:5-15).

In the same way, we invite spiritual death into our midst whenever we depart from His ordained way. Russell Lipton states it beautifully:

> *It is a settled principle of the (20th century) natural man to imitate the practices of other, idolatrous religions. The reason is simple. Christianity is the one way of life that cannot be carried out successfully by the natural man. It is spiritual through-and-through. It, quite literally, depends entirely on the Holy Spirit working through the renewed spirit, mind and will of believers . . . For this reason, church practice cannot be a matter of indifference ('it doesn't matter'), or, worse, an excuse for following the way of the world ('let's learn from the world's ways of building successful organizations and ask God to bless what we have already determined to do'). In a very real sense, the church is not on earth, nor is it like one of the nations. It does not follow from this that Biblical practice is impractical. Biblical practices are the most practical (the only practical) way that God can accomplish His will on earth. ("Detestable Practices," unpublished article)*

May we never forget Paul's warning regarding the subtle influence of empty philosophies that detract from Jesus Christ (Col. 2:8). Modern pragmatism is one of those philosophies. Because it has been baptized in the name of Christ, dressed in Christian garb, and concealed behind Biblical language, many modern believers assume that pragmatism is a Christian tenant.

Pragmatism boldly asserts that if something succeeds (according to human measurements) it must be right. Such thinking is spiritually perilous and Biblically invalid. Noah, Jeremiah, Isaiah, Ezra, Nehemiah, John the Baptist, Jesus, and the twelve apostles were all failures in the eyes of modern pragmatism!

In his penetrating essay called *Pragmatism Goes to Church*, A.W. Tozer goes to the heart of the matter:

What shall we do to break its [pragmatism's] power over us? The answer is simple. Acknowledge the right of Jesus Christ to control the activities of His church. The NT contains full instructions, not only about what we are to believe but what we are to do and how we are to go about doing it. Any deviation from those instructions is a denial of the Lordship of Christ. I say the answer is simple, but it is not easy for it requires that we obey God rather than man, and that brings down the wrath of the religious majority. It is not a question of knowing what to do; we can easily learn that from the Scriptures. It is a question of whether or not we have the courage to do it. (God Tells the Man Who Cares)

Whose House Are We Building?

Perhaps a simple illustration will help to underscore the force of what has been set forth in this chapter. Suppose that you hired a carpenter to build a den as an addition to your home. You sketched out a diagram specifying how you wanted the den to be built. You then carefully explained it to the carpenter.

After returning from a week long vacation, you were shocked to find that your new den barely resembled the pattern that you had sketched out. You then asked the carpenter why he failed to adhere to your plan. He responded by saying, "I thought my ideas were better than yours!"

Have we not done the same with *the Lord's* house!?

Regrettably, scores of Christians have had no qualms about rearranging the spiritual furniture in God's house without consulting the Owner. David is still placing the holy ark upon a Philistine cart. And Uzzah's human hand continues to try and steady it.

May we not be so unwise. The Lord help us to observe His "due order" (1 Chron. 15:13).

CHAPTER 11

WHAT SHALL YOU DO?

A common peril in the Christian walk is to equate a mental understanding of truth with living it out in real life. There exists a subtle danger of having a truth lie sterile in your intellect—mentally grasped but not spiritually applied.

Our problem is that we are rather quick to catch things in our minds while our experience lags far behind. Russell Lipton writes,

> *What we must guard against (and this applies with heaviest force to readers who do agree with this material) is mere mental assent to the church as an 'issue.' We live in a day of issues. Paul referred to issue-followers as those with tingling ears. He did not treat them gently. This church, this Bride for whom Christ as a heavenly suitor bore the cross, is no mere 'issue.' Around her completion revolves issues of life, death, reward, shame, heaven, hell. (Does the Church Matter?)*

Having a right perception of Divine things does not insure that we are holding them in our hands. With this thought in view, let us shift our focus to the challenging arena of practical application.

After you have made a fresh appraisal of the Biblical understanding of the church, you are no better off if you fail to flesh out the new light you have discovered. What you have read thus far has utterly dismantled your present understanding of the church. Now let me press the terse query: *What shall you do?*

Some have championed the idea of renewing the institutional church from the inside out. But those who have sought to revamp the established church have met serious resistance and frustration.

To be perfectly candid, unless the extra-biblical clergy/sectarian system is dismantled in a particular church, efforts to reach God's highest desire will be handcuffed. The following disheartening results will occur: The pastor will feel threatened. The staff will resist the disruption of the status quo. The congregation will be thrown into a panic. Individual believers will be utterly confused.

So before we discuss the Lord's answer to the problem of the contemporary church, let us take a brief look at some modern movements that have sought to renew it.

Shopping at a Supermall

The superstore megachurch trend is just one example of a failed attempt at renewing the church. These event-driven, shopping mall churches have created specialized boutiques for every sociological slice in America today. From single parents, twelve step recoverers, homebuilders, premarital couples, parents-of-adolescents, Generation Xers to working mothers, businessmen, actors, and dancers.

Advertised by extraordinarily gifted marketeers and driven by a formidable "growth-industry" mentality, megachurches attract thousands every Sunday into their enormous amphitheaters. They use the latest church growth strategies, organizational methods, and marketing techniques. It is no wonder that churches of this ilk are successful at swelling their ranks.

They provide flawless multimedia worship. They supply pep-rally like religious services. They offer high-tech visual effects. They possess tightly scripted gospel orations mingled with a heavy dose of comic relief.

They have seamless choreographed drama presentations. They attract frequent visits from featured celebrities whose clothes are always color-coordinated. They contain a zillion splinter interest groups designed to meet every consumer need.

To top it off, megachurches offer these mass-market religious resources to the public in exchange for minimal commitment, low visibility, and little cost. Stated simply, the megachurch movement is built on a corporate business paradigm that utilizes a market-driven approach to building the kingdom of God!

Unfortunately, those believers who are attracted to these large, flashy, organized Wal-Marts of the American religious world can hardly find a place in their hearts for a simple, unextravagant meeting centered around the person of Christ alone. To their minds, choosing between a lavish supermall church and a "house church" is like choosing between the flamboyant supercenter mall and the corner grocery store!

The weakness endemic to the superstore church is that it so emphasizes the "church scattered" dimension of the Body of Christ that the "church gathered" dimension suffers great loss. By focusing all attention on being "sensitive" to the comfort zones of "seeking" unbelievers, most megachurches have failed to adequately disciple their new converts into radical abandonment to Jesus Christ.

They have also failed to nurture close-knit communal relationships in the Body. What is more, the business machinery that drives these mammoth institutions obscures the organic nature of the church.

While it labors under the banner of "cultural relevancy," the supermall church bears too striking a resemblance to the shallow business structures of this age. It is for this reason that they do not have any profound or lasting impact on the culture.

Put plainly, the modern techniques the supermall church uses to communicate the gospel are as carnal as the system from which it is supposed to deliver people! In this way, the gospel has become trivialized, commercialized, and emptied of its power. It has been diluted as just another "product" in our consumer-obsessed culture.

In a word, the megamall church of modern pop-Christian culture bears little similarity to the simple, Spirit-dependent, Christ-centered, spiritually dynamic, mutually-ministering churches of the first century. And these were the churches that turned the world upside down (Acts 17:6)!

Pulled Under a Wave

The recent "third-wave movement" and its cousin, "the restoration movement," have been two highly influential players in the renewal game. (The Vineyard is the best noted denomination in the third-wave movement. MorningStar Ministries is well-noted in the restoration movement.)

Populated mostly by charismatics and Pentecostals, these movements stress the restoration of apostolic power. For brevity sake, I will call these related movements *third-wave-restoration.*

I have no quarrel with the pressing need for a genuine move of the Holy Spirit in and through the church today. But most third-wave-restoration churches have put the cart before the horse. Namely, they have sought to possess the power of the Spirit *before* they have gone under the flesh-severing knife of the cross.

Scripturally speaking, the cross is the exclusive ground for the Holy Spirit's power. Calvary preceded Pentecost. Our Lord's Jordan baptism preceded the arrival of the heavenly dove. The sacrificial altar preceded the heavenly fire. And the smitten rock preceded the flowing waters at Horeb.

So too the Holy Spirit only finds His resting place upon the altar of a crucified life. Recall the Lord's command to Israel not to pour the sacred oil upon any flesh (Exod. 30:32). This command is an apt figure illustrating how the cross cancels out the old creation. In short, the Spirit cannot work through uncrucified flesh!

The dangers of beginning with the Spirit rather than with the cross are numerous. For one thing, it can easily lead a person into an unwholesome quest for power without character.

Mystical experience without godliness. Unrestrained soulish excitement without sound discernment. And demonic counterfeits without spiritual reality.

Not a few Christians desperately seeking individual renewal are routinely packing their bags and flocking to the various "Christian Meccas" of revivalism sponsored by third-wave-restoration churches. These are folks who are desperate to be touched by God. So much so that they have become open targets for every new wind of doctrine or fad that blows through the doors of the church (Eph. 4:14).

(A new wind blows through the charismatic church about every five years. Christians eventually get burned out with it, and then look for another one to pick up. This is a never ending cycle.)

Many in the third-wave have developed an unhealthy dependence upon phenomenological experience. It is a dependence like that of an addict. They are driven to travel far and wide to acquire the next spiritual fix. Such dependence obscures the role of Scripture in the life of a believer. It equally fosters an unhealthy (and sometimes pathological) spiritual instability.

This is not to suggest that the third-wave-restoration movement has been without value to the Body of Christ. Indeed, the movement has contributed a number of helpful Biblical accents. Most significantly, it has fostered a genuine hunger for and openness to God's moving. It has produced a sound blending of evangelical and charismatic theology. And it has created a vast collection of wonderfully anointed worship and praise music.

But its basic flaws lie in its overemphasis on mystical experience; its tendency to put power *gifts* on the throne rather than Christ *the Giver*; and its zealous support of the modern clergy system. Quite frankly, the pastor is *king* in the typical third-wave-restoration church. Congregants who have been renewed with the new wine of the Spirit find very little freedom to fully function in their gifts during a typical third-wave service.

While third-wave-restoration churches may boast about possessing "the new wine," they have confined it to an old, leaking wineskin. A wineskin that inhibits mutual ministry, relatedness, freedom, and vibrancy. The old wineskin that is employed merely reinforces the "sit-and-soak" mentality that plagues the Body of Christ today.

"Christian guruism" is also epidemic in third-wave-restoration churches. High-powered "teachers," "prophets," and "apostles" are copious in the movement. They are revered as spiritual icons, basking in the limelight of fan-club followings.

A typical renewal crusade is similar to a rock concert where the featured celebrity gives an encore performance and takes his bow in the Christian limelight. It is not uncommon for third-wavers to arrive hours early to secure a prime seat to hear the latest circuit teacher who has come to town.

In effect, the third-wave-restoration movement has so emphasized the so-called "five-fold ministry" that it has rivaled and obscured the priesthood of all believers! It has stressed the *extra-local* ministry at the expense of *the local* church. And it is the latter that God has established to be the normal environment for individual spiritual nourishment.

It's no wonder that those who desire the fullness of God, but do not know first-century church life, are compelled to try anything that promises them a greater surge of renewal juice. Regrettably, many in the third-wave-restoration movement have rushed headlong toward spiritual ambiguity. They have whole-heartedly embraced a peculiar phenomenon that has little to no Biblical warrant. At the same time, they have shrugged their shoulders at a model for church life that has abundant Biblical merit.

Ironically, the very experience that multitudes in this movement are seeking to achieve can only be found in *ekklesia* life. When one tastes "Body life" as God has ordained it, they will be forever cured of the unbridled urge to travel "to and fro" to attend the latest "hot spot" of renewal. Instead, they will discover true and long-lasting refreshment and stability within the church. Those who wish to "chase God," therefore, will find Him in the *ekklesia*. For she is His highest passion.

To spin the metaphor, in seeking to ride the latest spiritual wave, many third-wave-restorationists have been caught in the undertow of a clergy-dominated ecclesiastical structure. As a result, some have been bitten by the sharks of counterfeit spiritual experience. They are now drowning in the murky waters of Christian mysticism and charismatic clericalism.

Sadly, CPR cannot be successfully administered within the institutional matrix of the third-wave-restoration movement. So the only hope for recovery lies in pulling the institutional plug to dispel the rising water.

Imprisoned in a Cell

Another attempt at renewal in recent years has been the emergence of the "cell church." Cell churches are based on a two-winged approach. They provide a weekly "cell group" meeting (set in a home) and a Sunday "celebration" meeting (set in a building).

The small cell meetings are designed for fellowship, ministry, prayer, and evangelism. The large group meetings are designed for preaching and corporate worship. There is much to be commended about the cell church movement. Namely, its emphasis on close-knit connectedness, one-anothering, and Body ministry. But its greatest weakness lies in its leadership style.

The cell church has left the unscriptural clergy system completely untouched! Native to cell churches is a top-heavy, hierarchical leadership structure that works against the community. Thus "the longer leash" is an apt metaphor to describe the cell church model!

The congregation is given a measure of church life as they meet together weekly at someone's home. Yet through a highly organized hierarchy, the pastor controls the gatherings and steers them according to his own wishes. (It's not uncommon for the "ministry time" in a cell meeting to be restricted to a discussion of the pastor's latest sermon!)

Moreover, in the typical cell church, the Sunday basilica service is treated as the prominent meeting. Cell church literature calls the cell "the basic unit" of the church. However, this is not what is ordinarily modeled.

Typically, the smaller cell meetings act as mere appendages. They chiefly serve as entry points for making the larger basilica church (to which the cells belong) increase in number. The cell church model looks impressive on paper. Cell church manuals are replete with elaborate flow charts and catchy organizational graphs. But it is found wanting in real life experience.

The cell church deserves our applause for its denunciation of "program-based" churches that find themselves mired in bureaucratic structures. But it warrants our disapproval for its blithe espousal of a rigid, multi-layered, hierarchical leadership structure.

Not only does this structure undermine Biblical principle, it also makes each cell an extension of *the pastor's* vision and burden! And it buries the believing priesthood under layers of human hierarchy.

Accordingly, the cell church model violates the very principle it claims to uphold: That the church is an organism made up of individual "spiritual cells." In stark contrast, each "cell group" is nothing more than a facsimile of the same Body part (the single pastor)!

Stated simply, the mere addition of home meetings (cells) to the clergy-dominated structure fails to go far enough in renewing the church. In a word, the cell church fails to express the full ministry of every believer and the functional Headship of Jesus Christ.

Adopting the Right Attitude

What I have said thus far is not meant to place judgment on any of God's dear people. It is rather meant to strike a contrast between those structures that God has sanctioned and those that He has not.

It is a fact that God has used and is using the institutional church. Because of His mercy, the Lord will work through any structure as long as He can find hearts that are truly open to Him. So there is no question that God is using cell, mega, and third-wave-restoration churches alike. (He is using them more than some so-called "house churches" that have grown insular and exclusive.)

But this is not the question at hand. The Lord holds us responsible for following His Word insofar as we have heard it. Comparing ourselves with others is shaky ground for seeking His approval (2 Cor. 10:12). Anything less than what God has disclosed in Scripture concerning church practice falls short of His full purpose. I do not say this judgmentally, but soberly. The words of T. Austin-Sparks capture the tone of my spirit:

> *While the sects and denominations, missions, and institutions are a departure from the Holy Spirit's original way and intention, God has undoubtedly blessed and used these in a very real way and has sovereignly done great work through faithful men and women. We thank God that it is so, and pray that every means possible of use may have His blessing upon it. This is not said in any patronizing or superior spirit: God forbid. Any reserve is only because we feel that there has been much delay, limitation, and weakness due to the departure from the first and full position of the first years of the church's life, and because of a heart-burden for a return thereto. We cannot accept the present 'disorder' as all that the Lord would or could have. (Explanation by T. Austin-Sparks of the Nature and History of 'This Ministry')*

The Symptom Masquerading as the Cause

Genuine church renewal requires that we distinguish between the *symptom* and the *root* of the problem. Elton

Trueblood has rightly said, "The basic trouble [with the institutional church] is that the proposed cure has such a striking
similarity to the disease" (*The Company of the Committed*).

Conferences for burned-out clergy, cross-denominational
unity gatherings, support groups for pastors who suffer from
"sheep bite," and workshops presenting the latest church growth
strategies are vivid examples of Trueblood's penetrating
observation. All of these supposed "cures" merely coddle the
system that is responsible for the church's maladies. They simply
treat the symptom while ignoring the real culprit. The result?
The same drama continues to play out on a different stage.

It is the clergy/sectarian system that inhibits the rediscovery
of face-to-face community, supplants the functional Headship of
Christ, and stifles the full ministry of every believer. Consequently, all attempts at renewal will be short-sighted until the
clergy structure and denominational system are dismantled in a
local fellowship. At best, such attempts will bring limited
change. At worse, they will invite open hostility.

To be blunt, the attempt to work for a recovery of the full
testimony of Jesus from the inside of an institutional church is a
worthless exercise. Such an attempt can be likened to the
dismantling of a tower from the ground. If those disassembling
the tower come close to compromising the structure, the tower
will fall down on them! The only way to dismantle a tower is to
proceed from the top down.

In like manner, modern churches will never reach God's end
if the clergy/denominational structure is not abandoned. For this
reason, renewal movements that merely transplant Biblical
principles into institutional soil will never succeed in realizing
the full purpose of God. In the words of Arthur Wallis,

> *A church is not fully renewed if the structures are left
> untouched. To have within a traditional church a live group
> composed of those who have received the Spirit and are
> beginning to move in spiritual gifts; to introduce a freer and
> livelier spirit into the worship with renewal songs; to permit*

the clapping and the lifting up of the hands and even to dance; to split the weeknight meeting into home groups for the purpose of discipling; to replace 'one-man leadership' with a team of elders—all these measures, good though they are, will only prove to be a patching operation. Individuals will undoubtedly be blessed. There will be an initial quickening of the church. But if it ends there, the long-term results will be detrimental. There will be a quiet struggle going on between the new measures and the old structures, and you may be sure the old structures will win in the end . . . the new patch will never blend in with the old garment. It will always look incongruous. (The Radical Christian)

In sum, the modern church will never be renewed until it recognizes that the framework with which it operates is inadequate and self-defeating. Despite the good intentions of the persons that populate it, the interior design of the institutional church sets us up for defeat.

True renewal, therefore, must be radical. That means it must go to the root! Recovering the Lord's testimony necessitates that we forsake our ecclesiastical patches and band-aids!

The Call to Leave Clergy-Dominated Christianity

I thank God for those Christians who have left their clerical professions, laid down their high-powered hierarchical positions, and abandoned their sects to become simple brethren in the Lord's house. It is among such that the Lord has found a clear basis for His own building.

As would be expected, those who have left their salaried, clergy positions have paid a tremendous cost. Such a thought strikes a sensitive chord in the heart of the average religious professional. For this reason many violently resist such a notion.

They react in a way not dissimilar to the silversmiths of Ephesus who withstood Paul's message because it "endangered their craft" (Acts 19:24-27). Unless those in clerical positions are ready to openly examine this issue before God, any discussion of the matter remains for them a highly flammable topic that can easily turn torrid.

Note that clerical leaders need not be despots in order to hinder mutual ministry. Most clergy are well-intentioned and gifted Christians who sincerely believe that God has called them to their profession. Some are highly stylized benevolent dictators. Others are spiritual tyrants with a Machiavellian quest for power. Such ones imprison and freeze the life of their congregations.

The point is that clergy need not use vicious forms of authority to be harmful to Body life. The mere presence of the one-up/one-down hierarchical mode of leadership suppresses mutual ministry. This is true regardless of how nonauthoritarian in temperament the clergyman may be.

The mere presence of clergy has the deadening effect of conditioning the congregation to be passive and perpetually dependent. Christian Smith makes the point perfectly:

> *The problem is that, regardless of what our theologies tell us about the purpose of clergy, the actual effect of the clergy profession is to make the Body of Christ lame. This happens not because clergy intend it (they usually intend the opposite) but because the objective nature of the profession inevitably turns the laity into passive receivers. The role of clergy is essentially the centralization and professionalization of the gifts of the whole Body into one person. In this way, the clergy represents Christianity's capitulation to modern society's tendency toward specialization; clergy are spiritual specialists, church specialists. Everyone else in the church are merely 'ordinary' believers who hold 'secular' jobs where they specialize in 'non-spiritual' activities such as plumbing, teaching, or marketing. So, in effect, what ought to be accomplished in an ordinary, decentralized, non-professional manner by all church members together is instead accomplished by a single, full-time profes-*

sional—The Pastor. Since the pastor is paid to be the specialist in church operations and management, it is only logical and natural that the laity begin to assume a passive role in church. Rather than contributing their part to edify the church, they go to church as passive receivers to be edified. Rather than actively spending the time and energy to exercise their gift for the good of the Body, they sit back and let the pastor run the show. ("Church Without Clergy," Voices in the Wilderness, Nov/Dec '88)

The average believer is probably unaware that his notion of leadership has been shaped by centuries of ecclesiastical history (about 1700 years worth!). In fact, the clergy concept is so embedded in our thinking that any attempt to deviate from it will meet fierce opposition.

For this reason most modern believers are just as resistant to the idea of dismantling the clergy as are clergy themselves. The words of Jeremiah have pertinent application: "The prophets prophesy falsely and the priests rule by their means; and *my people love to have it so*" (Jer. 5:31). "Clergy" and "non-clergy" alike are responsible for the ailments of the church.

Despising Not the Day of Small Things

Recall that in the history of Israel's captivity, God called His people out of Babylon to return to Jerusalem to rebuild His house. While Israel was in captivity in a foreign land, she still assembled to worship God in the various synagogues spread throughout the empire.

Yet the high call of God to Israel was to leave the comfortable homes she had erected in Babylon and return to Jerusalem to rebuild the Lord's true temple. Only a tiny remnant returned to the land (Ezra 9:7-8; Hag. 1:14). Most were unwilling to pay the price of leaving the convenient worship styles to which they had grown accustomed.

The call of God to Israel to leave Babylon foreshadows the present cry of the Spirit to His people today. Hear the burden of the prophet Haggai. His words reflect God's present call:

Is it time for you, O ye, to dwell in your ceiled houses, and this house lie waste? Now therefore thus saith the Lord of hosts; Consider your ways. Ye have sown much, and bring in little; ye eat, but ye have not enough; ye drink, but ye are not filled with drink; ye clothe you, but there is none warm; and he that earneth wages earneth wages to put it into a bag with holes. Thus saith the Lord of hosts; Consider your ways. Go up to the mountain, and bring wood, and BUILD THE HOUSE; and I will take pleasure in it, and I will be glorified, saith the Lord. (Hag. 1:4-8)

In view of the fact that only a small, seemingly insignificant remnant returned to Jerusalem to rebuild God's house, the prophet Zechariah issued this challenging rebuke: "*Who has despised the day of small things?*" Why did he issue such a word? Because despite the seemingly smallness of the endeavor, God was in it!

Despite the fact that most of Israel regarded the rebuilt temple "as nothing" in comparison to the surpassing splendor of the former temple, God was in it (Hag. 2:3)! Despite the fact that the elders of Israel wept in despair when they saw the tiny remnant lay down the unimpressive foundation, God was in it (Ezra 3:12)!

From Gideon's army of 300 to Elijah's 7,000 who had "not bowed the knee to Baal"—from the Levitical priests who first entered the promised land to the hidden Annas and Simeons of our Lord's day who "looked for the consolation of Israel"—God's most precious work has been accomplished through the small, the weak, and the unnoticed (1 Cor. 1:26-29; 1 Kings 19:11-13).

Success in the eyes of the world is tied to natural measurements. Numbers, extent, size, weight, etc. are all signs of success to the worldly minded. Yet the greatest things in God's eyes are exceedingly small in the eyes of men. George Moreshead insightfully asks,

> *Is there another stream running even more deeply and more hiddenly these days among the members of the Body, a scattered people who are being taken into the depths of the revelation and experience of Christ in the most extreme measures of the Holy Spirit's dealings, emptying, crucifying . . . a pioneer company which the Lord will need for the opening of the way for the remainder of the Body to follow—perhaps some 'eleventh-hour laborers' now in the process of His producing? (Excerpt from a personal letter to the author)*

Along this same line, T. Austin-Sparks writes,

> *What is called 'Christianity'—and what has come to be called 'the church'—has become a tradition, an institution, and a system quite as fixed, rooted, and established as ever Judaism was, and it will be no less costly to change it fundamentally than was the case with Judaism. Superficial adjustments may be made—and are being made—but a very heavy price is attached to the change which is necessary to really solve the great problem. It may very well be, as in the time of the Lord, that the essential light will not be given to very many because God knows that they would never pay the price. It may only be a 'remnant'—as of old—who will be led into God's answer because they will meet the demands at all costs. (Quoted from an unpublished manuscript authored by George Moreshead)*

Let it be clear. The call of God to recover the primitive simplicity of first-century church life requires that we begin on an entirely new ground. A ground different from the religious systems and customs that fallen men have constructed. And that ground is Jesus Christ!

But this does not answer our initial question of what we shall do. It simply clears away the brush so that we can see the field of God's purpose more plainly. Scripture does not offer us any ready-made steps for the building of a first-century styled church. But it does supply us with several broad principles that are essential to any work that is seeking to recover God's fullest thought. They are—

(1) A Fresh Revelation

Proverbs 29:18 says, "Where there is no revelation, the people cast off restraint" (NIV). Before any attempt can be made to gather according to God's intention, it is imperative that we first receive a fresh vision of the church as God sees it.

This vision must spring from a new seeing of the Person of Jesus Christ. For the church is none other than Christ in corporate expression! Such a "heavenly vision," as Paul called it, is indispensable to building the Lord's house (Acts 26:19). For the church is built upon the revelation of Jesus Himself (Matt. 16:15-18).

The revelation of Christ is the hub of everything in the spiritual path. And the whole NT is built upon it. It is through the revelation of the Lord Jesus that we are born again (Matt. 16:17); that we are transformed into His image (2 Cor. 3:18); that we are equipped for Christian work (Gal. 1:16); and that our bodies will be gloriously translated (1 John 3:2).

Our whole Christian life—from its inception to its consummation—rests upon a continuous, full-orbed vision of the Risen Christ to our hearts by the Holy Spirit. And it is only when our hearts are captivated by a revelation of Jesus in His splendor that we can receive a vision for His work.

As was the case with Moses, the tabernacle can only be built after we have been shown its pattern from above. That pattern is

Christ. In short, we need a vision *of* the Lord before we can receive a vision *for* the Lord. Russell Lipton remarks,

> *Paul prayed that the Ephesians would receive a revelation in the knowledge of Christ and have the eyes of the heart opened. This is our great need . . . Why has the church that Christ longs for been so misunderstood, so perverted, so opposed? It is due entirely to the blindness of we His people. Without revelation, how can you act? With revelation, you will know what to do (Does the Church Matter?)*

We desperately need a ground-breaking, Spirit-inspired, matchless revelation of Christ and His church. Such a vision given from the heavenly throne is the very springboard for God to raise up a testimony that reflects His fullest thought for His beloved children. It is the necessary precondition for true renewal in the Body of Christ.

(2) A Paradigm Shift

To borrow a term from scientific philosopher Thomas Kuhn, we need a "paradigm shift" regarding the church before we can properly build it. That is, we need a new world view regarding the meaning of the Body of Christ. A new model for understanding the *ekklesia*. A new framework for thinking about the church. Of course, the "new paradigm" that I am speaking of is not new at all. It is the paradigm that undergirds the entire NT.

Our day is not much different from that of Nehemiah's. In that day, Israel had rediscovered the law of God. They had been without it for many years. Once discovered it had to be re-explained and re-interpreted. Nehemiah 8:8 says, "So they read in the book in the law of God distinctly, and *gave the sense*, and *caused them to understand the reading.*"

In the same way, 20th-century Christians must re-learn the language of Scripture with respect to the church. The original meaning of countless Biblical terms like "church," "minister," "pastor," "house of God," "ministry," and "fellowship" have been largely lost. Such misunderstandings have eroded the landscape of the church.

These words have been invested with institutional power. A power that was foreign to those who originally penned them. Therefore, a pressing need in the church today is the rediscovery of Biblical language. Joseph Higginbotham and Paul Patton ardently make the point:

> *Let's face it: our language reflects our practice. It is hard to get people to occupy the ground of universal priesthood when we reserve the word 'minister' for people with seminary degrees and parchment paper ordination certificates . . . Linguistic gymnastics have changed the Christ who heads a whole and unified Body into the tribal god of a denomination or of a local church. It has to do with how we've been using the word 'church.' We seldom use it the way Christ used it. We speak of 'building a church,' when we should be saying that we are erecting a new building where Christ's people can meet. We speak of 'starting a church,' when we should speak of affirming, in a given locale, the church which Christ is already building. ("The Battle for the Body," Searching Together, Vol. 13:2)*

Most American Christians have learned to read their NTs through the modern lens of 20th-century institutionalism. Hence, there is an urgent need for us to rethink our entire concept of church and learn to see it afresh through the lens of the NT authors.

Because of common misteaching, we have many deeply buried assumptions that are in need of excavation and examination. We have been mistaught that "church" means a building, a denomination, or an organizational structure. And that a "minister" is a special class of Christian.

Since our contemporary notion of the church has been so entrenched in man's thinking, it requires a conscious effort to view it in the way that all first-century Christians did. It demands that we rigorously plough through the thick and tangled weeds of human tradition until we unearth the virgin soil of spiritual reality.

Only the necessary task of rethinking the church in its Scriptural context will enable us to distinguish between the Biblical notion of church and those institutions that pose as churches. Let us briefly isolate some of those differences:

The Institutional Paradigm	The Biblical Paradigm
◆ is sustained by a clergy system	◆ knows nothing of a clergy system
◆ seeks to energize the laity	◆ doesn't recognize a separate class called laity
◆ renders the bulk of its congregants passive-in-their-pews	◆ makes all members functioning priests
◆ associates church with a building or a denomination that one "joins"	◆ affirms that people do not *go to* church nor *join* the church . . . affirms that they *are* the church
◆ is rooted in unifying those who share a special set of customs or doctrines	◆ is rooted in unreserved fellowship with *all* Christians based on Christ alone
◆ thrusts "ordinary" Christians out of the holy of holies and chains them to a pew	◆ liberates all believers to serve as ministers in the context of a non-clerical, decentralized form of church leadership
◆ places its priority on religious programs and keeps its congregants at arms-length, insulating them from one another	◆ places its priority on face-to-face, shared-life relationships, mutual submission, openness, freedom, mutual service, and spiritual reality—the very elements that were built into the fabric of the NT church
◆ spends most of its resources on building expenditures and pastor-staff salaries	◆ spends most of its resources on "the poor among you" and apostolic workers

♦ operates on the basis that the pastor/priest is the functional head (while Christ is the nominal head)

♦ operates on the basis that Christ is the functional Head through the invisible guidance of the Holy Spirit through the believing community

♦ enshrines and protects the clergy-dominated, program-centered system that serves as the driving machine of the organized church

♦ shows a revulsion for the clergy system because it quenches the sovereign exercise of the Holy Spirit (yet lovingly embraces every Christian within that system)

♦ builds *programs* to fuel the church; views people as cogs in the machine

♦ builds *people* together with Christ to provide the momentum for the church

♦ encourages believers to participate institutionally and hierarchically

♦ invites believers to participate relationally and spiritually

♦ separates church(ecclesiology) from personal salvation (soteriology); views the former as a mere appendage to the latter

♦ forges no link between personal salvation and the church; sees the two as inextricably intertwined. (Scripture has it that when people were saved, they simultaneously became part of the church and immediately met together.)

To make the point better by someone else, the Biblical paradigm represents "the winning back to God of things ordinary and the desacralisation of things made sacred by human hands."

Because the traditional paradigm has been so entrenched in the minds of so many Christians, the mere notion of "coloring outside the lines" of this model is quite terrifying. The unfortunate result is that those who have not had a paradigm shift regarding the church will either ignore or oppose those churches that have.

In the eyes of those who see the world through institutional glasses, unless a church meets in the "right" place (a building), has the "proper" leadership (an ordained pastor or priest), and bears the "correct" name (one that indicates a "covering"), it is not an authentic church! Instead, it is dubbed with innovative terms like "para-church."

For those who have not yet grown weary of running on the program-driven treadmill of institutional "churchianity," that which is abnormal is considered normal. And that which is normal is regarded as abnormal. This is the unhappy result of not basing our faith and practice upon Scripture. In making this same point, Jon Zens shows a wealth of insight saying,

> *It seems to me that we have made normative that for which there is no Scriptural warrant (emphasis on one man's ministry), and we have omitted that for which there is ample Scriptural support (emphasis on one another) . . . we have exalted that for which there is no evidence, and neglected that for which there is abundant evidence. ("Building Up the Body: One Man or One Another?," Searching Together, Vol. 10:2)*

In like manner, Alexander Hay laments the dilemma of the contemporary church saying,

> *Tertullian found it necessary to say, 'Custom without truth is error grown old.' There is not a little in our modern church order and practice that has no Scriptural warrant. Yet because it has long been the custom, it is accepted without question as an essential part of Divine order. (NT Order for Church and Missionary)*

Most Christians have given careless adherence to humanly-devised traditions and tightly-held paradigms regarding church structure. Hence, any fresh way of doing church is viewed with unreasonable suspicion. This is true even if that way has far more Biblical undergirding than the ill-fated traditional model.

In brief, nothing short of a paradigm shift regarding the church coupled with an impartation of fresh light from the Holy Spirit will produce enduring change. Readjustments to the old wineskin, no matter how radical, will only go so far.

In other words, the church does not need *renewal.* It needs *replacement*! The only way to renew the institutional church is to wholly disassemble it and build something far different! The brittle wineskin of church practice and the tattered garment of ecclesiastical forms need to be exchanged, not just modified.

What is needed is a *new* wineskin and a *new* garment (Luke 5:36-38)! What is needed is a paradigm shift (on a natural plane). What is needed is a fresh revelation of Christ and His church (on a spiritual plane).

May you be delivered from carelessly imposing *your* pattern of church organization upon the NT authors. And may you have the courage to discard our institutional baggage. Or at least be willing to open your bags and inspect the luggage!

(3) The Centrality and Supremacy of Christ

The birth of a first-century styled church requires the labor pains of a company of people who embrace the centrality and supremacy of Jesus Christ with utmost rigor. In order for God to fulfill His ultimate intention, He needs a people who are jealous for the exclusive Headship of His Son.

Christ Himself must be the foundation and the superstructure (1 Cor. 2:2; 3:11; Eph. 2:20). He must be the center of the church. The issue of Christ's supremacy lies at the core of why the church is such a provocative and confusing issue today. Because the church is so inextricably intertwined with Christ's sovereign Headship, the forces of darkness have waged a relentless onslaught against it. This warfare is centered on keeping our eyes blinded to the true meaning of the *ekklesia.*

When we see the Lord on His throne, we begin to see the church. For the two are inseparably interwoven. In a word, we cannot build the *Body* if we fail to embrace the *Head*!

By the same token, if we discover NT principle for church life without coming to grips with the demands of Christ's Headship, we shall suffer great loss. Rather than meeting upon the basis of Jesus Christ, we will meet on something lesser.

(4) Counting the Cost

King David was a man who denied Himself so that God could obtain what He wanted. David writes,

I will not enter my house or go to my bed—I will allow no sleep to my eyes, no slumber to my eyelids, till I find a place for the Lord, a DWELLING for the Mighty One of Jacob. (Ps. 132:3-5, NIV)

The Lord will never birth a fresh expression of His Body if we are not willing to pay the price that is attached to it. Among other things, we must refuse to compare ourselves with other Christians and measure our success by their standards.

The peril of ancient Israel rested in its willingness to follow the multitudes that surrounded it. By contrast, we must learn to connect our obedience to what God has revealed to our own hearts through Scripture. (Not to what the rest of His people are doing.) In Exodus 23:2, the Lord warned Israel about the peril of following after the multitudes. This warning holds good for us today.

If God has shown us the church, He holds us responsible for responding to what we have seen. Nothing short of unreserved obedience to the heavenly vision will provide the necessary context for the Spirit to raise up a local expression of His Body.

Unfortunately, not a few Christians familiar with the NT have side-stepped the Lord on this issue. The following trite excuse reflects the common thinking on the subject: "God will sort out the problem of the church someday. I'm just going to support the institutional churches until something big happens."

Such a fatalistic mentality conceals our own rebellion. It is also a profound intellectual failure. It is easy to take refuge in the true but irrelevant conviction that "God will sort it all out in the end." It is much more difficult to do the hard work of discovering and responding to God's will. Such an attitude is similar to saying, "I will not obey until I see others obeying." Truly, to hold such an attitude is to court the displeasure of the Lord.

Let it be clear. There is a price to pay in obeying the Lord's prescribed way for His church. You will have to reckon with being misunderstood by those who have embraced institutional, spectator Christianity. You will bear the marks of the cross and die a thousand deaths in the process of being built together with other believers in a close-knit community.

You will have to endure the messiness that is part and parcel of relational Christianity—forever abandoning the artificial neatness afforded by the organized church. You will no longer share the comforts of being a passive spectator. Instead, you will learn the self-emptying lessons of becoming a responsible, serving member of a functioning Body.

In addition, you will have to go against the harsh grain of what one writer calls "the seven last words of the church" (*we never did it that way before*)! You will incur the disfavor of the religious majority for refusing to be influenced by the tyranny of the status quo. Finally, you will incite the severest assaults of the adversary in his attempt to snuff out that which represents a living testimony of Jesus. But regardless of the suffering that follows those who take the road less traveled, the glorious benefits of living in Body life far outweigh the costs.

Unless we are a crucified people, there can be no true expression of the church. It is a settled spiritual principle that the church issues from the cross. Just as the altar preceded the house in the Old Testament, the cross always precedes the church. So unless a people are willing to go under the cross corporately, they will never see the church restored.

It is for this reason that not a few groups that have left the institutional church have seen short lives. Whenever a company of believers makes something other than Christ the basis for their gathering, it loses the Headship of Christ. And it will find itself in the death throes of disintegration.

This is true for groups that make "NT order" the basis for their meeting. It is also true for groups that gather out of a negative reaction. A reaction that can be likened unto a group of religious malcontents waging a "holy" crusade against institutional Christianity. Such groups have succumbed to the false mentality that they are the only ones doing church correctly.

These groups end up becoming inverted communities. Elitist, cloistered, and ingrown. Poisoned with pride. Their meetings are characterized by the same chord of criticism against "the religious system." And they eventually die for lack of positive vision.

The essential elements that will hold a church together under severe testing are: 1) holding fast to the Headship of Jesus in a living way, and 2) a perpetual self-emptying for the Lord's sake. Without the practical working of the cross in our lives, *ekklesia* life becomes no more than a far-reaching ideal.

The Lord builds on broken lives. His house is constituted out of conflict (1 Chron. 26:27). This being the case, "let us, then, go to Him outside the camp, bearing the disgrace He bore" (Heb. 13:13, NIV). For it is there that we may match the Savior's heartbeat.

(5) Travailing Prayer

Finally, and most importantly, the church is restored among those who have learned to touch the throne of God with travailing prayer. The first church was born by a group of 120 disciples who devoted themselves to such prayer (Acts 1:13-15). NT expressions of the Body of Christ are formed the same way today.

We must never forget that the church is organic. It cannot be constructed by the hasty impulses of the natural man. The birthing of a church requires the kind of travailing prayer that marked the lives of Nehemiah and Daniel.

These men entered into prayerful travail over the present disorder in which they lived. As a result, God was faithful to bring others to stand by them. Only then did He fulfill the vision He deposited within their hearts (Neh. 1-2; Dan. 9-10).

Prayer, then, is critical for receiving the power of the Spirit. A power that is necessary for birthing and nurturing a local expression of the Body of Christ. Again, the church is not made with the hands of human clay. It is made by the breath of the Eternal Spirit.

Recall how the temple of old was built without the sound of earthly machinery (1 Kings 6:7). This incident establishes a crucial principle. Namely, that the church of Jesus Christ can never be formed by the toil and sweat of the natural man. It must be birthed from heaven. In the words of Russell Lipton,

It is only by the Holy Spirit that the church is built, not by the cleverness of our schemes and plans and committees and campaigns. We are often too clever to admit that we depend on our own strength rather than on the Holy Spirit . . . but we do. (Does the Church Matter?)

If we are willing to be deeply involved in the battle locally for those elements that reflect God's end and God's way, He will be faithful to respond. Paul's prescription for church building sums it up rather nicely: "My little children, of whom I *travail in birth* again until Christ be formed in you" (Gal. 4:19). In this light, John W. Kennedy remarks,

The extent to which God can use us to the establishing of the church is the extent of our subjection to Him, and our freedom from the bonds of tradition and other human entanglements which would hinder His working. Then the church will not need to be cajoled into existence. The Spirit Himself will bring to birth the urge that brings an assembly into being . . . erecting a building, or establishing the observance of the Lord's Table or a certain mode of gathering has never yet made a church. Without a burning vision of the Lord's way, and the urge of the Spirit to obey, any pattern will remain but an empty sham. (The Secret of His Purpose)

Travailing prayer does not rule out the undisputable fact that God uses men to plant His church. That the first-century church was built through apostolic ministry is a consistent practice throughout the NT. Strikingly, every church mentioned in Scripture was either directly planted or immensely helped by a traveling worker. It is a Divine pattern.

Therefore, believers who enter into travailing prayer should seek the help of an apostolic worker (or "church planter") who will lay the foundation for the new church. Apostolic workers are God's instrument for imparting a revelation of Jesus Christ to the hearts of men. They are the ones specially called and gifted by God to lay the foundation.

If we will be true to NT principle, then, we will accept the role of such people. For without apostolic ministry, we will never see a restoration of God's house. (See *So You Want to Start a House Church?* for details on the role of itinerant workers.)

A Final Call

We live in an hour when the Spirit of God is beckoning His people to embrace His ultimate intention regarding His beloved church. This intention rests upon forming a people who are filled with the new wine of God's Spirit for the single purpose of preparing them to be a glorious Bride for His Son. Within this context, He is summoning His people to re-examine the old wineskin of church practice.

Therefore, the need of the hour is for the Lord to raise up multitudes of those in the spirit of the sons of Issachar who "had understanding of the times and knew what Israel [God's people] ought to do" (1 Chron. 12:32). George Moreshead explains,

In these times when doing (even if doing 'for God' and 'for His glory') has so largely eclipsed the Biblical emphasis on, and the priority of, being and becoming, it would seem to be equally necessary and important to have those with the spiritual understanding and discernment to know what the NT 'Israel' ought both to do and not to do! How then can there be anything to rival, as the primary need of the present time, the raising up of those who see from heaven—believers of exceptional spiritual stature and a Spirit-taught understanding of this time, for the building up of the Body of Christ to the measure of Christ's fullness? How else can the 'old men' of the new 'Israel' join in with their younger brethren in the song of victory and the shout of success over God's completed house? ("Understanding the Times," unpublished article—slightly paraphrased)

In closing, I trust that what I have attempted to set forth in this book will provoke you to no longer dilute the wine of spiritual life and confine it into old wineskins. But rather, that you will be ignited by a blinding vision of the *ekklesia*.

My closing prayer is that the sweet wine of the Spirit would pour so mightily that the wineskins of man's making—which have obscured the Headship of Jesus and disarmed the believing priesthood—would burst beyond recovery! I pray that God would raise up countless local expressions of dynamic spiritual life all across the globe. Expressions that live simply and serve sacrificially for the realization of His eternal purpose. May you be counted faithful to be a part of this passing parade!

The Lord help you to rethink the wineskin.

APPENDIX: THE NEXT STEP

If you have rightly understood the message of this book, you have arrived at two stirring conclusions.

1) the institutional church has no Scriptural right to exist.
2) the Lord's best and highest for you as His child is that you get plugged into a first-century styled church.

If you have come to these two conclusions, a major decision awaits you. A crisis of conscience, if you will. The question before the house is: "Now that I have seen that God does not own the institutional church, am I willing to make a clean break with it?"

If your answer is "yes," then you have resolved half the battle. You will be making your exodus out of something that does not reflect God's highest purpose. But the question of *how* and *what* you are supposed to enter into still remains.

Some folks try to resolve this dilemma by starting their own house church. They step out of the institutional church one day and open their home for meetings the next. But such a step lacks just as much Scriptural backing as does starting an institutional church! Not to mention that it does not work.

Beginning a *genuine* first-century styled church is one of the most difficult things that can be done. It takes much time, much ministry, and much experience to get a group of Christians to function in a living way under Christ's Headship. Training them to deal with the myriad of problems that they will encounter as a face-to-face community is just as challenging.

As is the case with all functions in the Body, God has not called everyone to plant house churches (1 Cor. 12:17-18, 28-30). Instead, He has specially called, equipped, and seasoned some for this enormous task (Acts 13:2; Eph. 4:11).

What, then, is the next step?

I refer you to read my book *So You Want to Start a House Church?* It discusses how the churches of the first century were planted. More importantly, it gives readers who wish to begin meeting in NT-fashion a practical answer to the question: "What shall I do now that I have left the institutional church?"

This book spells out the next step!

Just go to **www.ptmin.org/start.htm** to order it.

Go to **www.ptmin.org/pagan.htm** to order the companion volume to *Rethinking the Wineskin* which traces the historical (and unbiblical) origins of our modern-day church practices.

BIBLIOGRAPHY

The following bibliography includes the principal publications quoted in this book as well as a number of other related titles that deserve comment.

NT Church Practice

Atkerson, Steve, ed. *Toward a House Church Theology*, NT Restoration Foundation. Includes some thoughtful essays on first-century church practices. Available from NTRN, 2752 Evans Dale Circle, Atlanta, GA 30340.

Austin-Sparks, T. *God's Spiritual House,* Testimony Book Ministry. Illuminating discussion of the chief spiritual features of the church. Available from Emmanuel Church, 12,000 East 14th St., Tulsa, OK 74128.

Banks, Robert. *Going to Church in the First Century*, SeedSowers. Insightful reenactment of a first-century styled church meeting drawn from superb scholarship.

_____. *Paul's Idea of Community*, Hendrickson. Scholarly yet readable discussion of the early house churches mentioned in the NT.

Banks, Robert and Julia. *The Church Comes Home*, Hendrickson. Great discussion of the practical outworking of house church.

Bonhoeffer, Dietrich. *Life Together*, Harper & Row. Meaningful discussion of the spiritual underpinnings of Christian community.

Congdon, Dana. *Recovery and Restoration: Two Views of God's End-Time Work,* Christian Tape Ministry. Excellent comparison of the restoration and recovery movements of church renewal. Available from the publisher at 4424, Huguenot Road, Richmond, VA 23235

Edwards, Gene. *Beyond Radical*, SeedSowers. Explores the unbiblical origins of many of our modern church traditions. Unfortunately, this book is neither documented nor footnoted.

_____. *Climb the Highest Mountain*, SeedSowers. Terrific discussion about handling division, strife, and crisis in the church.

_____. *How to Meet in Homes*, Seedsowers. Superb discussion on how churches were planted in the first century and how they should be planted today.

_____. *Revolution: The Story of the Early Church*, SeedSowers. Masterful portrayal of the church in Jerusalem during the first seventeen years.

_____. *The First Century Diaries,* Tyndale. Wonderful historical-fictional account of the early church, from South Galatia to Rome.

_____. *When the Church Was Led Only By Laymen*, SeedSowers. Enlightening discussion about leadership in the early church.

Foster, Harry. *The Church as God Wants it Today*, Testimony Book Ministry. Challenging and refreshing look at God's thought for His church.

Freeman, Bill. *The Church is Christ*, Ministry of the Word. Christocentric view of the church.

Giles, Kevin. *What on Earth is the Church? An Exploration in NT Theology*, InterVarsity Press. Insightful look at the corporate and communal dynamics of the early church.

Girard, Robert C. *Brethren, Hang Loose*, Zondervan. Outstanding account detailing the dynamic underpinnings of NT Body life.

_____. *Brethren, Hang Together*, Zondervan. Marvelous discussion about restructuring the church for relational fellowship under the Headship of Jesus.

Gish, Arthur. *Living in Christian Community*, Herald Press. Seminal work on the practical dimensions of the church as a community.

Hay, Alexander R. *NT Order for Church and Missionary*, NT Missionary Union. Classic volume on the NT pattern of church order.

Kaung, Stephen. *Recovery*, Christian Tape Ministry. Examines God's work in this hour with respect to the church. Available from the publisher at 4424 Huguenot Road, Richmond, VA 23235.

Ketcherside, W. Carl. *The Twisted Scriptures*, Diversity Press. Well-written discussion about the peril of division in the Body of Christ.

Kokichi, Kurosaki. *Let's Return to Christian Unity*, SeedSowers. Excellent treatment of the true meaning of Christian unity.

Kraus, Norman C. *The Community of the Spirit: How the Church is in the World*, Herald Press. Effective discussion about how the church is a new covenant community that lives a distinct life from the world by the Spirit's presence.

Lang, G.H., *The Churches of God*, Schoettle Publishing. Thorough discussion about the major principles that govern the local expression of the Body of Christ. Available from Lewis Schoettle Publishing, P.O. Box 1246, Hayesville, NC 28904.

Lee, Witness. *How to Meet*, Living Stream Ministry. Spiritual look at church meetings.

Lohfink, Gerhard. *Jesus and Community*, Fortress Press. Scholarly discussion of the early Christian idea and practice of community and its roots in the ministry of Jesus.

Loosely, Ernest. *When the Church Was Young*, SeedSowers. Hard-hitting comparison of the early church with the modern traditional church.

Miller, Hal. *Christian Community: Biblical or Optional?*, Servant Books. Outstanding discussion on the church in the light of God's central purpose.

Nee, Watchman. *The Normal Christian Church Life*, Living Stream Ministry. Virtual masterpiece on the work (of church planting) and its relationship to the church.

_____. *The Body of Christ: A Reality*, Christian Fellowship Publishers. Excellent work discussing the spiritual principles that govern the proper functioning of the Body of Christ.

Pethybridge, W.J. *The Lost Secret of the Early Church*, Bethany Fellowship. Concise but powerful appeal to return to the simplicity of first-century styled church meetings.

Smith, Christian. *Going to the Root*, Herald Press. Outstanding presentation of nine practical proposals for radical church renewal.

Snyder, Howard A. *Radical Renewal: The Problem of Wineskins Today*, Touch Outreach Ministries. Effectively discusses the meaning and implications of Biblical church renewal.

_____. *The Community of the King*, InterVarsity Press. Incisive look at the church and its relationship to God's eternal purpose.

Sterrett, Clay. *Myths of the Ministry*, CFC Literature. Good discussion outlining three common but mistaken notions of "the ministry." Available from the publisher at P.O. Box 245, Staunton, VA 24401.

Svendsen, Eric. *The Table of the Lord: An Examination of the Setting of the Lord's Supper in the NT and it's Significance as an Expression of Community*, NT Restoration Foundation. One of the best books available on the subject. Technical yet readable.

Thornton, L.S. *The Common Life in the Body of Christ*, Dacre Press. Scholarly masterpiece focusing on how the Body of Christ is a spiritual, communal reality.

Trotter, Dan. *New Reformation Review*. Radical, witty, and provocative newsletter advocating the house church concept. Available at www.geocities.com/Athens/Academy/8395/

Trueblood, Elton. *The Company of the Committed*, Harper & Row. Excellent discussion about the Biblical dynamic of community.

_____. *The Incendiary Fellowship*, Harper & Row. Classic consideration of the meaning and import of Biblical fellowship.

Viola, Frank. *From Nazareth to Patmos: The Saga of the First-Century Church*, Present Testimony Ministry. Tells the entire story of the early church from beginning to end. Found at www.ptmin.org

_____. *So You Want to Start a House Church?* Present Testimony Ministry. Discusses how churches were planted in the first-century. It is the next step after reading *Wineskin*. Found at www.ptmin.org

_____., et al. *The House Church Movement: Which Direction Will it Take?* Seedsowers. Boldly spells out what is missing and needed in the modern house church movement.

_____. *Who is Your Covering? A Fresh Look at Leadership, Authority, and Accountability*, Present Testimony Ministry. A companion to *Rethinking*, it explores the subjects of leadership, authority, and accountability in greater detail.

Wallis, Arthur. *The Radical Christian*, Cityhill Publishing. Challenging look at Biblical church renewal as envisioned in the NT. Available from the publishers at 4600 Christian Fellowship Road, Columbia, MO 65203.

Zens, Jon, ed. *Searching Together,* Word of Life Church. Superb magazine dealing with NT church practices and matters of doctrinal truth. Available from *Searching Together*, P.O. 377, Taylor Falls, MN 55084.

_____. *The Pastor,* Word of Life Church. Fog-clearing discussion about what the Biblical idea of a pastor is and isn't.

OTHER BOOKS

Volume 2: Who is Your Covering? A Fresh Look at Leadership, Authority, and Accountability. This book explores the issues of church leadership and spiritual authority in much more depth than *Wineskin*.

Volume 3: Pagan Christianity: The Origins of Our Modern Church Practices. A unique work that traces every modern Protestant practice, proving that it has no root in the NT.

Volume 4: So You Want to Start a House Church? First-Century Styled Church Planting. A must read after completing *Rethinking the Wineskin*. This book discusses the apostolic pattern for planting NT-styled churches. It also answers the question: "What shall I do now that I have left the organized church?"

Volume 5: From Nazareth to Patmos: The Saga of the New Testament Church. A synopsis of the entire story of the first-century church in its chronological, historical, and social context.

The Untold Story of the New Testament Church: An Extraordinary Guide to Understanding the New Testament. A detailed re-telling of the entire story of the first-century church in chronological order. This book gives the entire background to each letter in the NT.

Knowing Christ Together. A unique and insightful discussion on walking with the Lord with other believers.

Straight Talk to Elders. A thorough and compelling survey from Matthew to Revelation on the role and function of first-century elders and pastors.

For these titles and more, visit our ever-growing web site: **www.ptmin.org.**

To correspond with the author or to obtain further information about first-century styled church life, email **PTMIN@aol.com**